The Complete Guitar Player
Acoustic Songbook

Published by:
Wise Publications
14-15 Berners Street, London W1T 3LJ, UK.

Compiled and edited by Toby Knowles.
Music processed by shedwork.com
Cover designed by Fresh Lemon.

EXCLUSIVELY DISTRIBUTED BY

The A Team Ed Sheeran 6

Ain't No Sunshine Bill Withers 4

Annie's Song John Denver 9

Brown Eyed Girl Van Morrison 12

California Dreamin' The Mamas And The Papas 15

The Cave Mumford & Sons 18

Chasing Pavements Adele 22

Don't Know Why Norah Jones 25

Don't Panic Coldplay 28

Dream Catch Me Newton Faulkner 30

Every Rose Has Its Thorn Poison 33

Father And Son Cat Stevens 36

Fields Of Gold Sting 39

Fifty Ways To Leave Your Lover Paul Simon 46

Folsom Prison Blues Johnny Cash 42

Friday I'm In Love The Cure 44

Hallelujah Jeff Buckley 49

Hey, Soul Sister Train 52

Ho Hey The Lumineers 55

Homeward Bound Simon & Garfunkel 60

I Will Wait Mumford & Sons 63

Imagine John Lennon 58

The Joker Steve Miller Band 66

Jolene Dolly Parton 70

Knockin' On Heaven's Door Bob Dylan 68

Lay, Lady, Lay Bob Dylan 73

Let It Be The Beatles 76

Life On Mars? David Bowie 79

Love Story Taylor Swift 82

Make You Feel My Love Adele 86

Mrs. Robinson Simon & Garfunkel 88

Ordinary World Duran Duran 91

Redemption Song Bob Marley 94

Rocket Man Elton John 96

Romeo And Juliet Dire Straits 99

Save Tonight Eagle-Eye Cherry 102

The Scientist Coldplay 104

Sing Travis 107

The Sound of Silence Simon & Garfunkel 116

Space Oddity David Bowie 110

Stand By Me Ben E. King 114

Tears In Heaven Eric Clapton 119

Torn Natalie Imbruglia 122

Vincent (Starry Starry Night) Don McLean 124

The Weight The Band 128

Wild World Cat Stevens 131

Wonderwall Oasis 134

Yesterday The Beatles 140

You're Still The One Shania Twain 137

You've Got A Friend James Taylor 142

Ain't No Sunshine

Words & Music by Bill Withers

1.

Am⁷

2. Won-der this__ time where she's

2.

Am

And I know, I know, I know,__ I know,

N.C.

I know, I know, I know, I know, I know I know, I know, I know, I know, I know, I know,__

__ I know, I know, I know, I know, I know, I know, I know, I know, I know, I know, I

know, hey,__ I ought to leave the young thing a - lone,__ but, ain't no sun - shine when she's

Am⁷   Em   G   Am⁷

D.S. al Coda

gone._____ Ain't no sun - shine when she's

Coda

Am

Em⁷   G   Am⁹

An - y- time__ she goes a - way.

The A Team

Words & Music by Ed Sheeran

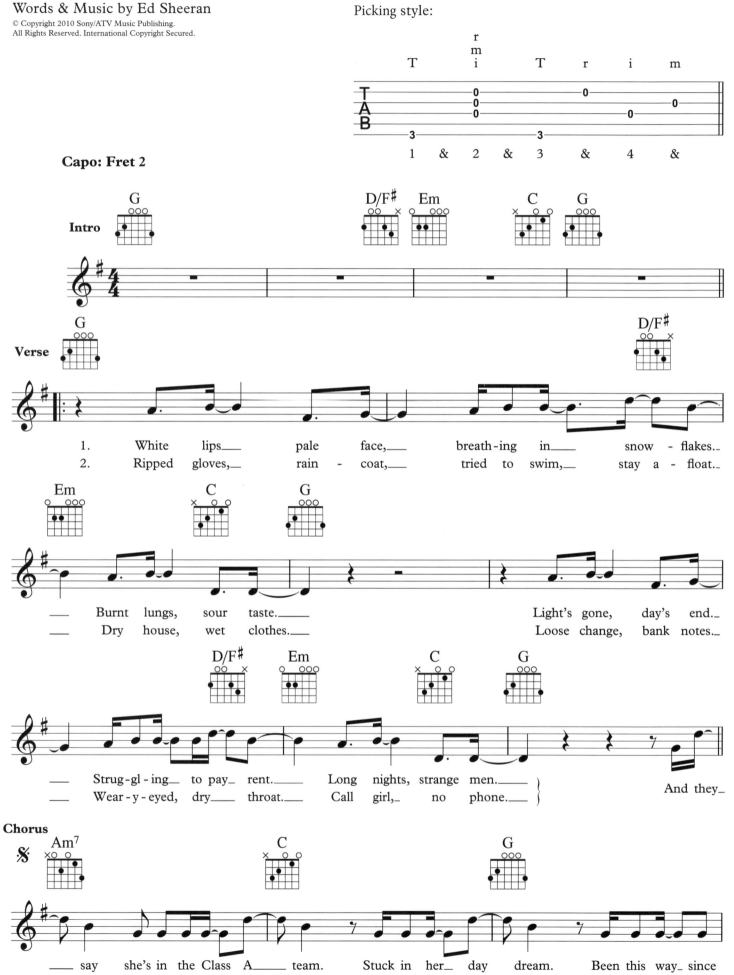

Annie's Song

Words & Music by John Denver

Picking style:

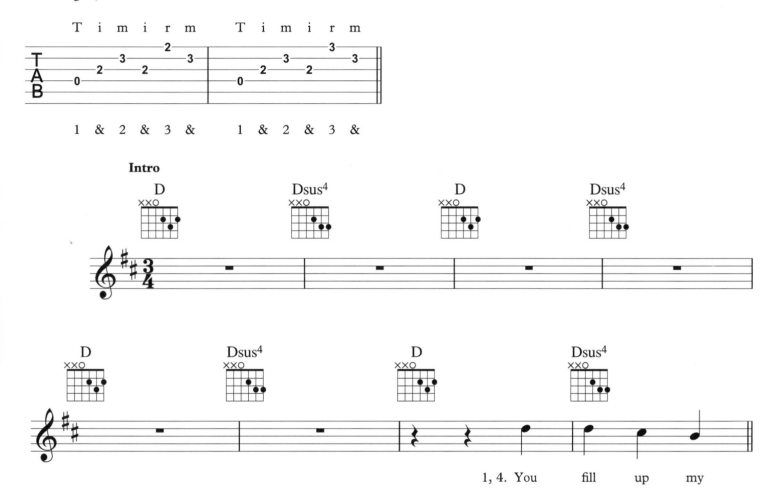

- gain.

- gain.

- gain.

2. Come, let me

3. Mm, mm,

4. You fill up my

⊕ Coda

(4.) des - ert, like a sleep - y blue

o - cean; you fill up my

sen - - ses, come, fill me a -

- gain.

Brown Eyed Girl

Words & Music by Van Morrison

Strumming style:

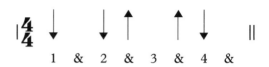

Try to memorise the chord sequence. That way, you can concentrate on the sound, rather than reading, when you play this song.

1. Hey where did   we   go,   days__ when the rains__ came?
2. What - ev - er   hap-pened   to Tues-day and so_____ slow?
3. So hard to find my way   now__ that I'm all   on my own.

Down__ in the hol - low,__   play - in' a new__
Go - in' down__ the old mine with a   tran - sis - tor ra -
I saw you just the oth - er day,   my, how you have__

____ game.   Laugh - in' and a - run - nin', hey,__ hey,
-di - o.   Stand - in' in the sun - light laugh - in',
____ grown.   Cast my mem - 'ry back there, Lord,__

12

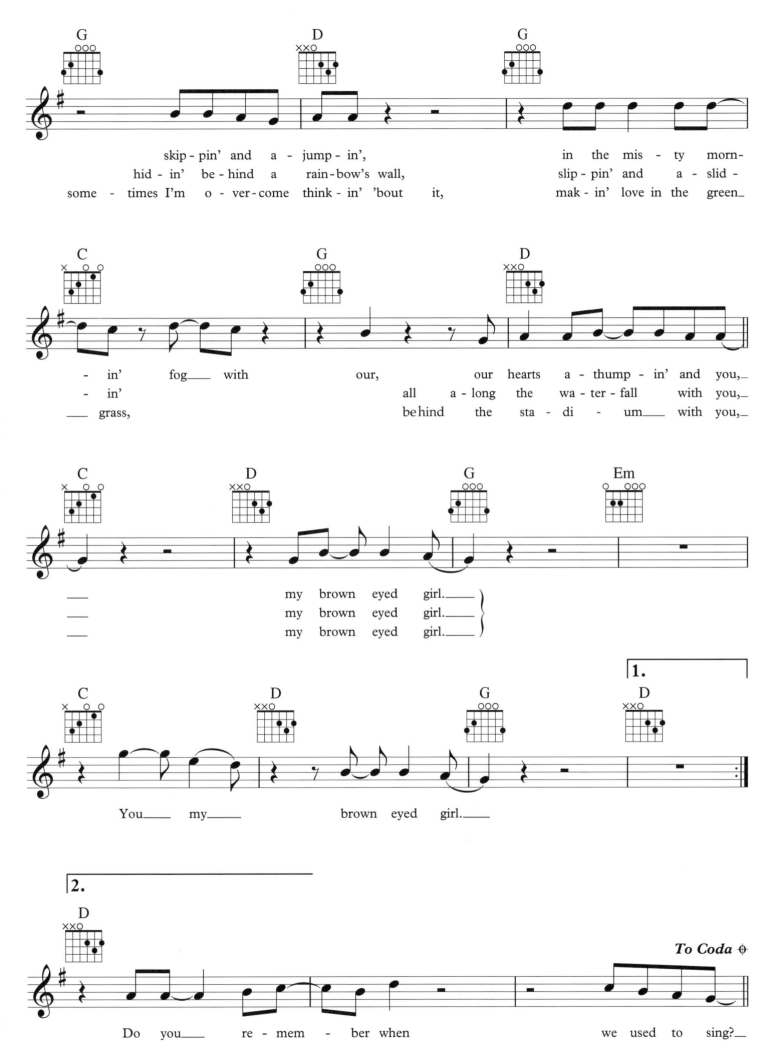

skip - pin' and a - jump - in',
in the mis - ty morn-

hid - in' be - hind a rain-bow's wall,
slip - pin' and a - slid -

some - times I'm o - ver - come think - in' 'bout it,
mak - in' love in the green___

- in' fog___ with our,
our hearts a - thump - in' and you,___

- in'
all a - long the wa - ter - fall with you,___

___ grass,
be - hind the sta - di - um___ with you,___

___
my brown eyed girl.___

___
my brown eyed girl.___

___
my brown eyed girl.___

1.

You___ my___ brown eyed girl.___

2.

To Coda ⊕

Do you___ re - mem - ber when
we used to sing?___

Chorus

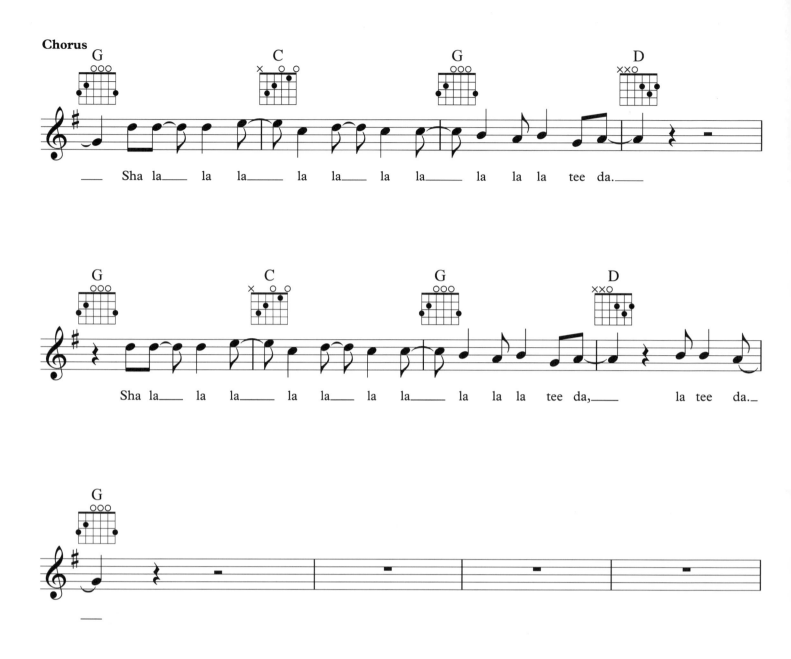

Sha la la la la la la la la la la tee da.

Sha la la la la la la la la la la tee da, la tee da.

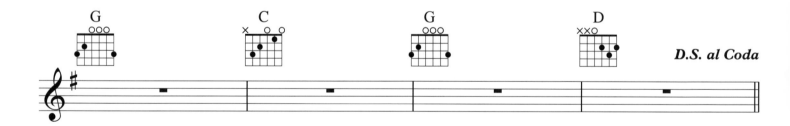

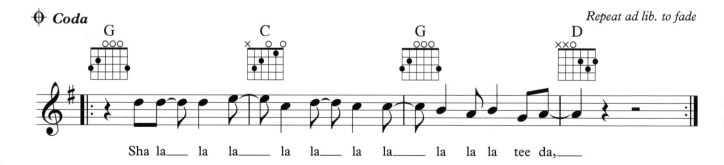

Repeat ad lib. to fade

Sha la la la la la la la la la la tee da,

California Dreamin'

Words & Music by John Phillips & Michelle Gilliam

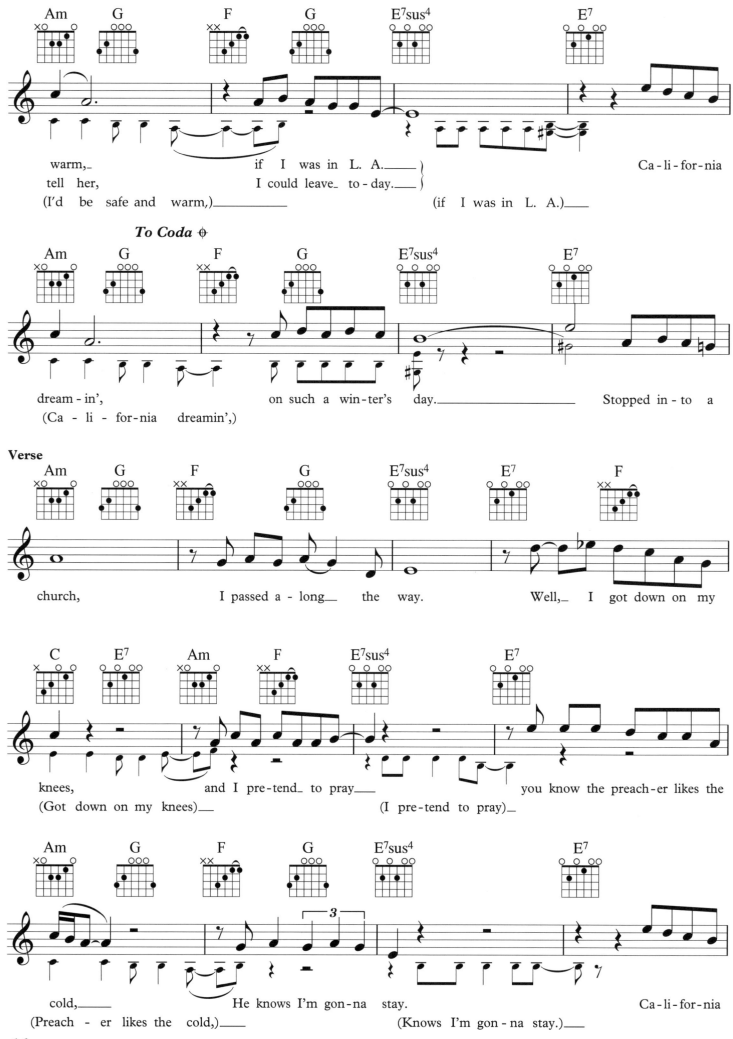

warm,—   if I was in L. A.——⟩   Ca-li-for-nia
tell her,   I could leave— to-day.——⟩
(I'd be safe and warm,)———————   (if I was in L. A.)——

To Coda ⊕

dream-in',   on such a win-ter's day.———————————— Stopped in-to a
(Ca-li-for-nia dreamin',)

Verse

church,   I passed a-long— the way.   Well,— I got down on my

knees,   and I pre-tend— to pray——   you know the preach-er likes the
(Got down on my knees)—   (I pre-tend to pray)—

cold,——————   He knows I'm gon-na stay.   Ca-li-for-nia
(Preach-er likes the cold,)——   (Knows I'm gon-na stay.)——

16

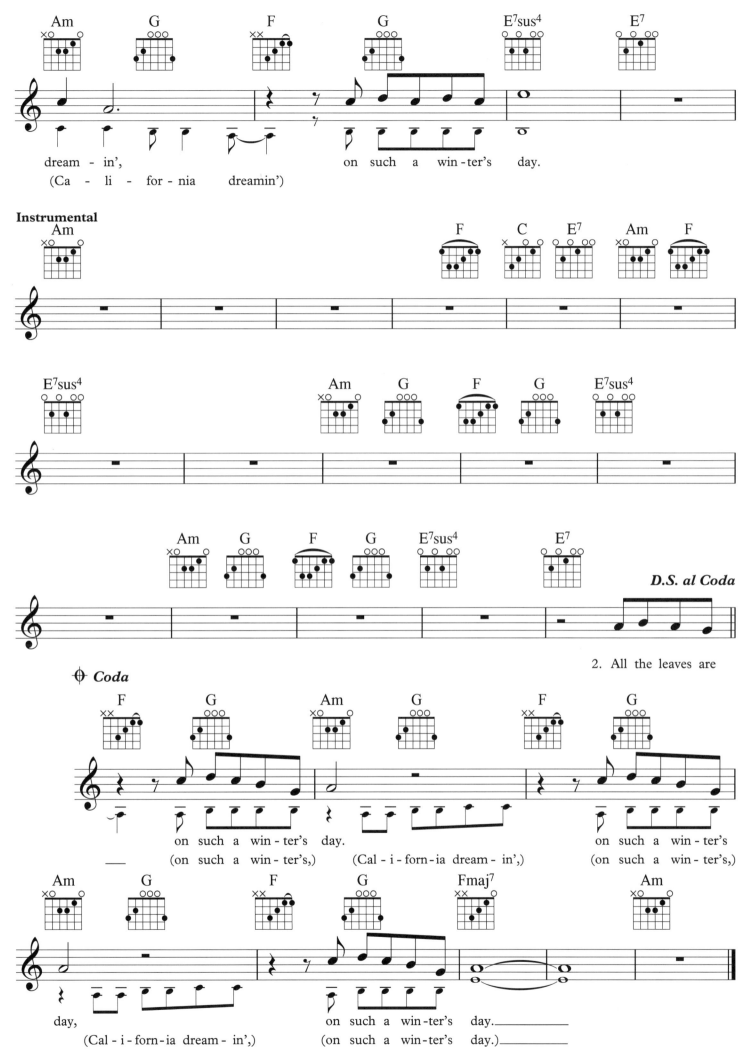

Instrumental

D.S. al Coda

2. All the leaves are

Coda

17

The Cave

Words & Music by Mumford & Sons

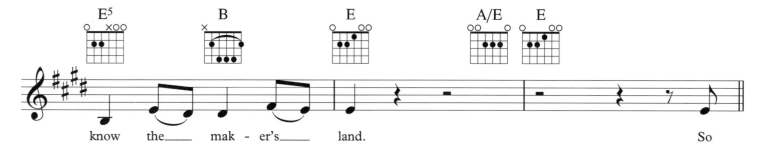

know the___ mak - er's___ land. So

Chorus

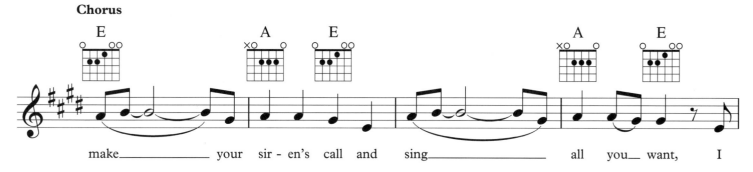

make_____ your sir - en's call and sing_____ all you__ want, I

will not hear what you have to say. 'Cause I_____ need free - dom now and

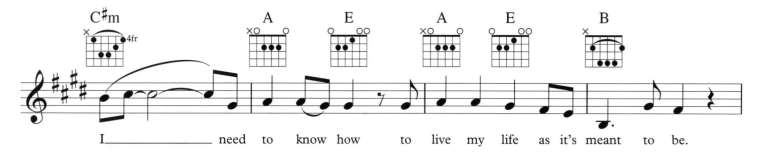

I_____ need to know how to live my life as it's meant to be.

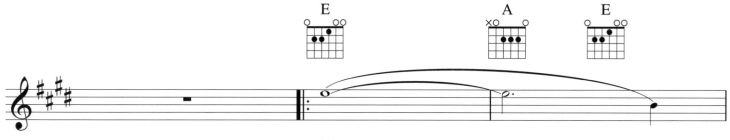

(Ah,_____

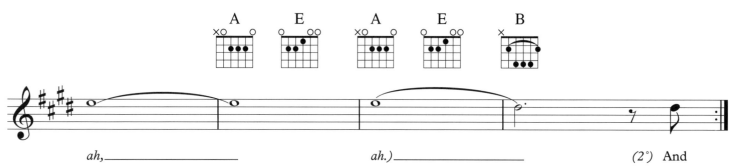

ah,_____ ah.)_____ (2°) And

Verse 2
The harvest left no food for you to eat,
You cannibal, you meat-eater, you see.
But I have seen the same,
I know the shame in your defeat.

Verse 3
'Cause I have other things to fill my time,
You take what is yours and I'll take mine.
Now let me at the truth,
Which will refresh my broken mind.

Verse 4
So tie me to a post and block my ears,
I can see widows and orphans through my tears.
And know my call despite my faults
And despite my growing fears.

Chasing Pavements

Words & Music by Adele Adkins & Eg White

Arpeggio style:

Try this picking pattern throughout the intro and first verse; then switch to a simple strumming pattern for contrast.

Capo: Fret 3

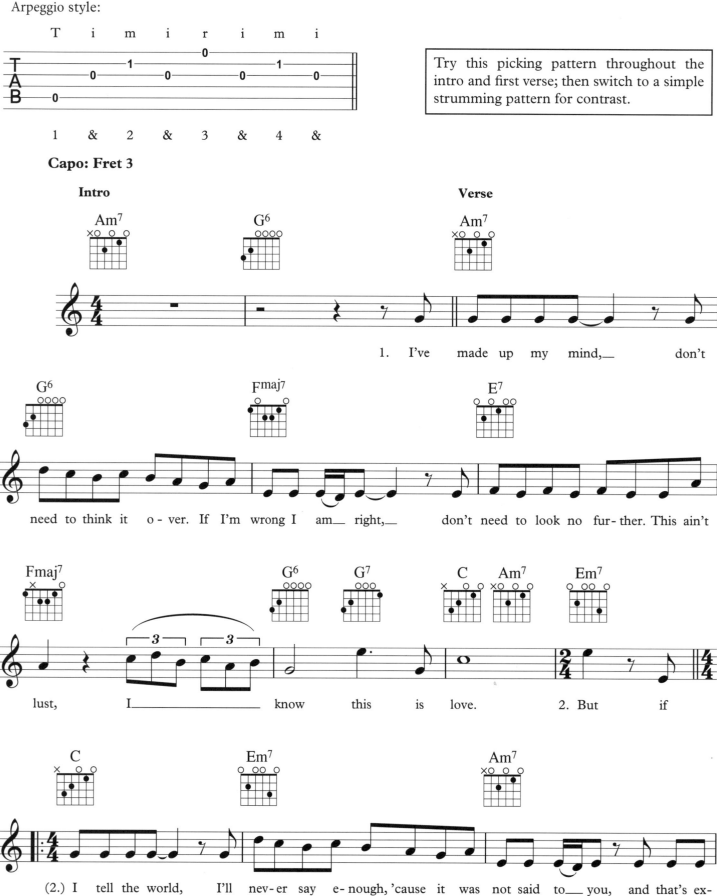

1. I've made up my mind,— don't need to think it o-ver. If I'm wrong I am— right,— don't need to look no fur-ther. This ain't lust, I_____ know this is love. 2. But if

(2.) I tell the world, I'll nev-er say e-nough, 'cause it was not said to— you, and that's ex-
(3.) build my-self up— and fly a-round in cir-cles, wait-ing as my heart drops and my

Bridge

Fmaj⁷   Em⁷   Dm⁷

Should I give up? Or___ should I just keep chas-ing pave-ments e - ven if it leads no-

G⁶   Fmaj⁷   E⁷

- where?___ Or___ would it be a waste e - ven___ if I knew my place? Should I___ leave it

D⁹   Gsus⁴   Fmaj⁷   Em⁷   Am⁷

there?___ Should I_____ give up?_____ Or should I just keep on chas-ing___

D.S. al Coda

Dm⁷   Fmaj⁷   Em⁷   Am⁷   Dm⁷   Fmaj⁷   G⁷

pave-ments? Should I just keep on chas-ing___ pave-ments? Or_____

⊕ *Coda*

Em⁷   C

leads no - where?_____

24

Don't Know Why

Words & Music by Jesse Harris

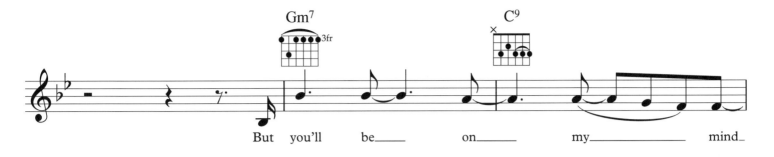

But you'll be___ on___ my___ mind___

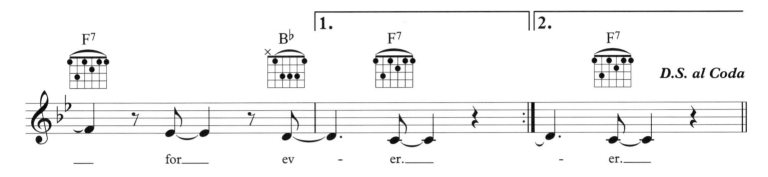

1. **2.**

D.S. al Coda

___ for___ ev - er.___ - er.___

Coda

don't know why___ I did - n't come. I___

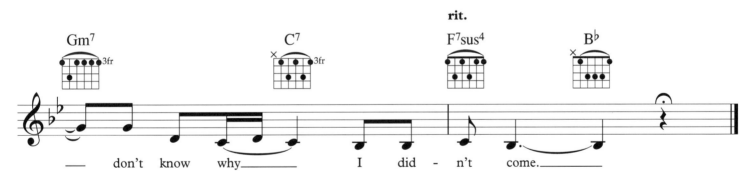

rit.

___ don't know why___ I did - n't come.___

Verse 3:
Out across the endless sea,
I will die in ecstasy.
But I'll be a bag of bones,
Driving down the road alone.

Chorus:
My heart is drenched in wine, etc.

Verse 4:
Something has to make you run,
I don't know why I didn't come.
I feel as empty as a drum,
I don't know why I didn't come,
I don't know why I didn't come,
I don't know why I didn't come.

Don't Panic

Words & Music by Guy Berryman, Chris Martin, Jon Buckland & Will Champion

Dream Catch Me

Words & Music by Crispin Hunt, Gordon Mills & Newton Faulkner

Strumming style:

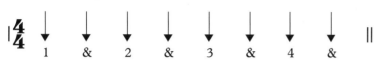

Capo: Fret 7

Chorus

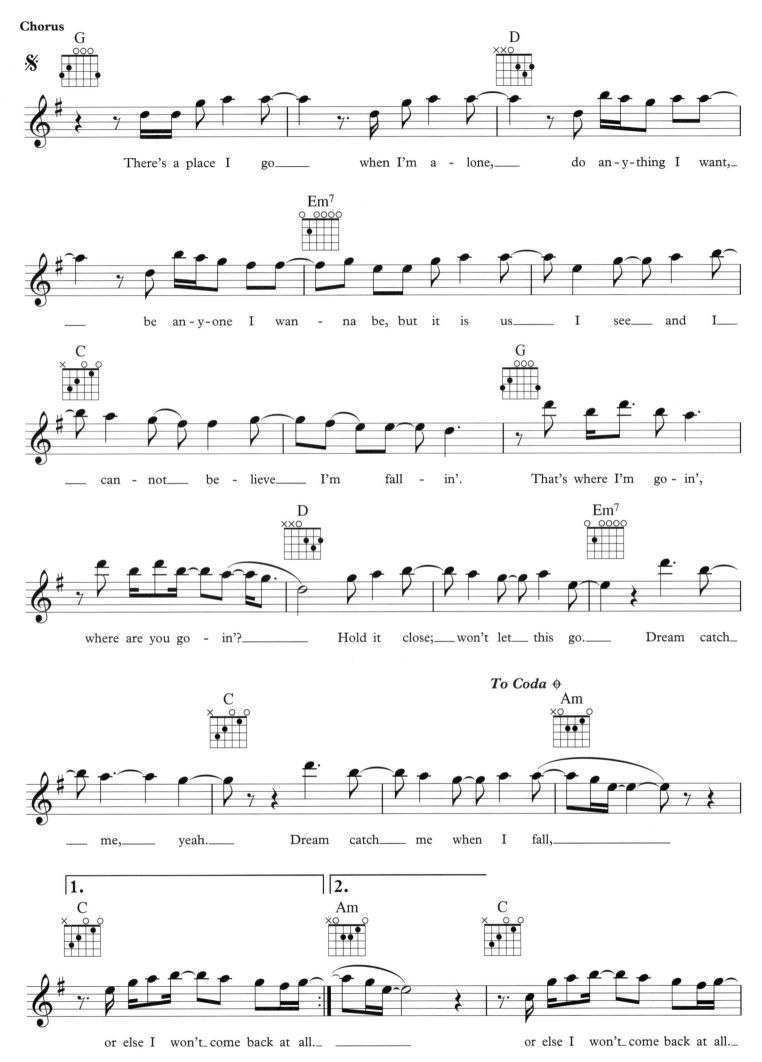

There's a place I go_____ when I'm a - lone,_____ do an-y-thing I want,__

__ be an-y-one I wan - na be, but it is us_____ I see__ and I__

__ can - not__ be - lieve_____ I'm fall - in'. That's where I'm go - in',

where are you go - in'?_____ Hold it close;__won't let__ this go.__ Dream catch__

To Coda ✛

__ me,_____ yeah._____ Dream catch__ me when I fall,_____

1.

or else I won't__come back at all.__ _____

2.

or else I won't__come back at all.__

Bridge

See you as a moun - tain, a foun - tain, a God.___ See you as a des-

- cant soul___ in the set - ting sun. You as a sound,___ just as si - lent as none,___

___ I'm___ yours._____ There's a place I go___ when I'm a - lone,___

___ do an - y - thing I want,___ be an - y - one I wan - na be. But it is us___

D.S. al Coda

___ I see___ and I___ can - not___ be - lieve___ I'm___ fall - in'.

Coda

or else I won't___ come back at all.___

Every Rose Has Its Thorn

Words & Music by Bret Michaels, Bruce Johannesson, Robert Kuykendall & Richard Ream

Strumming style:

The strumming is based on sixteenth-notes (four per beat). Leaving out certain strums, as shown, creates an interesting rhythm.

To match original recording, tune down one semitone.

1. We both lie si-lent-ly still___ in the dead of the night. Al-though we both lie close to-ge-ther, we feel miles a-part___ in-side.___ Was it some- -thing I said or some-thing I did,___ did my words___ not come out right? Though I tried___ ___ not to hurt___ you,___ though I tried...___ But I guess_ that's why___ they say: Ev-

33

Chorus

- 'ry rose_ has its thorn,___ just like ev - 'ry night_ has its dawn,_

_____ just like ev - 'ry cow - boy sings his sad,_

__ sad_ song:_ Ev - 'ry rose has its thorn.__ Yeah, it does.

lis - ten to our fav- 'rite song,_ play-ing on the ra - di - o,____ hear the D.-

3. I know I could have saved a love that night if I'd known what to say.

- J. say__ love's a game_ of ea - sy come and ea - sy go.___ But I won-

'Stead of ma - kin' love we both made our sep -'rate ways. And now I

- der, does he__know? Has he ev - er felt__ like this?_ And I know__

hear you found some - bo- dy new and that I ne -ver meant that much to you. To hear_

Father And Son

Words & Music by Cat Stevens

Intro:

In the intro, 'hammer on' to C/G: strum down on G on the 2nd beat, then change chord shape without strumming again.

To match original recording, tune down one semitone.

1. It's not

time to make a change,__ just re - lax, take it ea - sy. You're still
(2.) once like you are now,__ and I know that it's not ea - sy to be

(Verse 4 see block lyrics)

young, that's your fault,__ there's so much you have__ to know. Find__ a girl,__
calm when you've found__ some - thing go ing on._____ But take your time,__

_____ set - tle down,__ if you want____ you__ can mar - ry. Look at me,__
_____ think a lot,__ think of ev - 'ry - thing__ you've got,__ for you will

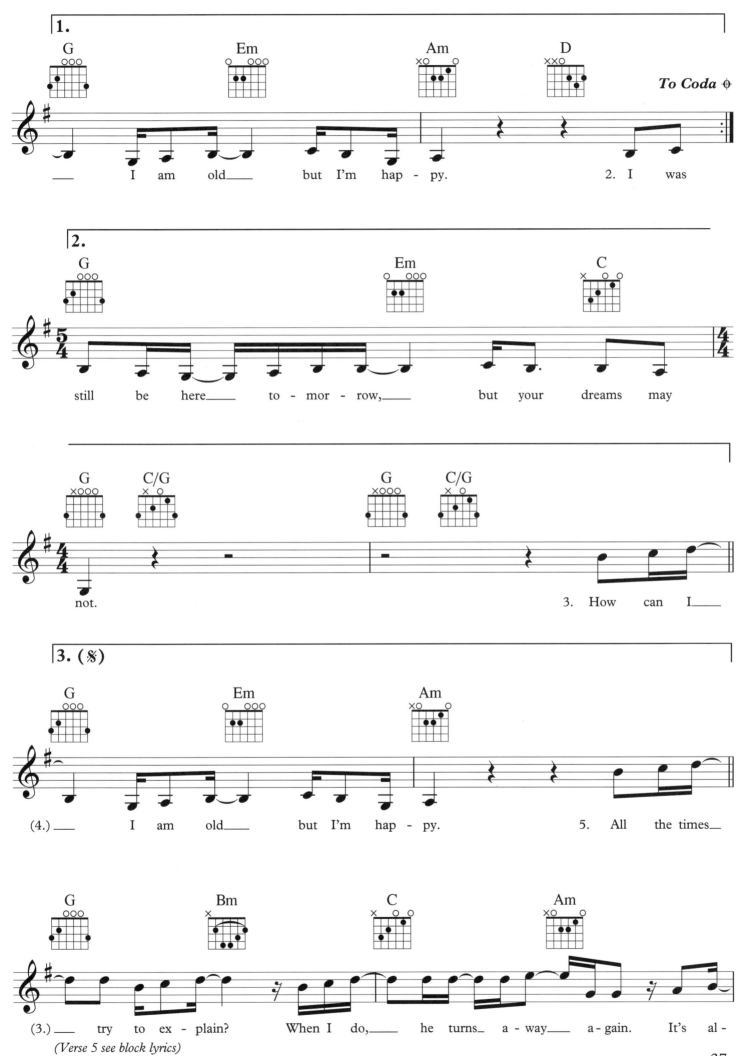

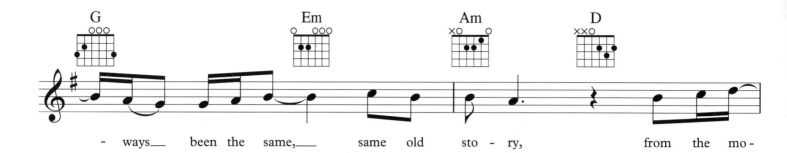

- ways___ been the same,___ same old sto - ry, from the mo -

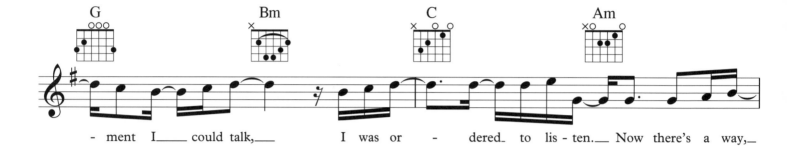

- ment I___ could talk,___ I was or - dered_ to lis - ten.__ Now there's a way,__

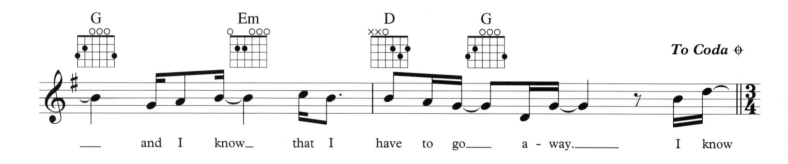

___ and I know_ that I have to go___ a - way._____ I know

To Coda

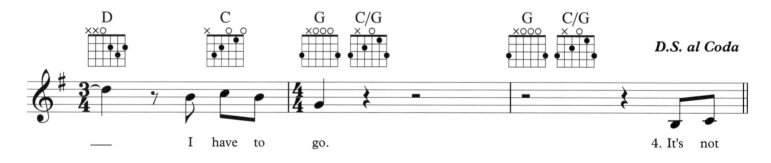

___ I have to go. 4. It's not

D.S. al Coda

Coda

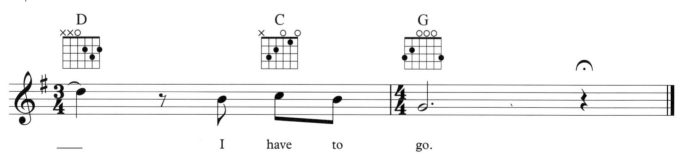

___ I have to go.

Verse 4:
It's not time to make a change,
Just sit down, take it slowly.
You're still young, that's your fault,
There's so much you have to go through.
Find a girl, settle down,
If you want you can marry.
Look at me, I am old but I am happy.

Verse 5:
And all the times that I've cried,
Keeping all the thing I knew inside,
It's hard, but it's harder to ignore it.
If they were right, I'd agree,
But it's them they know, not me,
Now there's a way,
And I know I have to go away.
I know I have to go.

Fields Of Gold

Words & Music by Sting

-on the fields___ of bar - ley. In his arms she fell as her
-on the fields___ of bar - ley. Feel her bo - dy rise when you

hair came down a - mong___ the fields_ of gold. Will you
kiss her mouth a - mong___ the fields_ of gold.

Bridge

I nev-er made pro-mi-ses light - ly and there have been some that I've bro - ken,

but I swear_ in the days still left we'll walk___ in fields_ of gold.

We'll___ walk in fields_ of gold.

Instrumental

40

Folsom Prison Blues

Words & Music by Johnny Cash

Strumming style:

> Alternate the bass notes between the root note and the fifth of the chord: that's between the 6th & 5th strings for E.

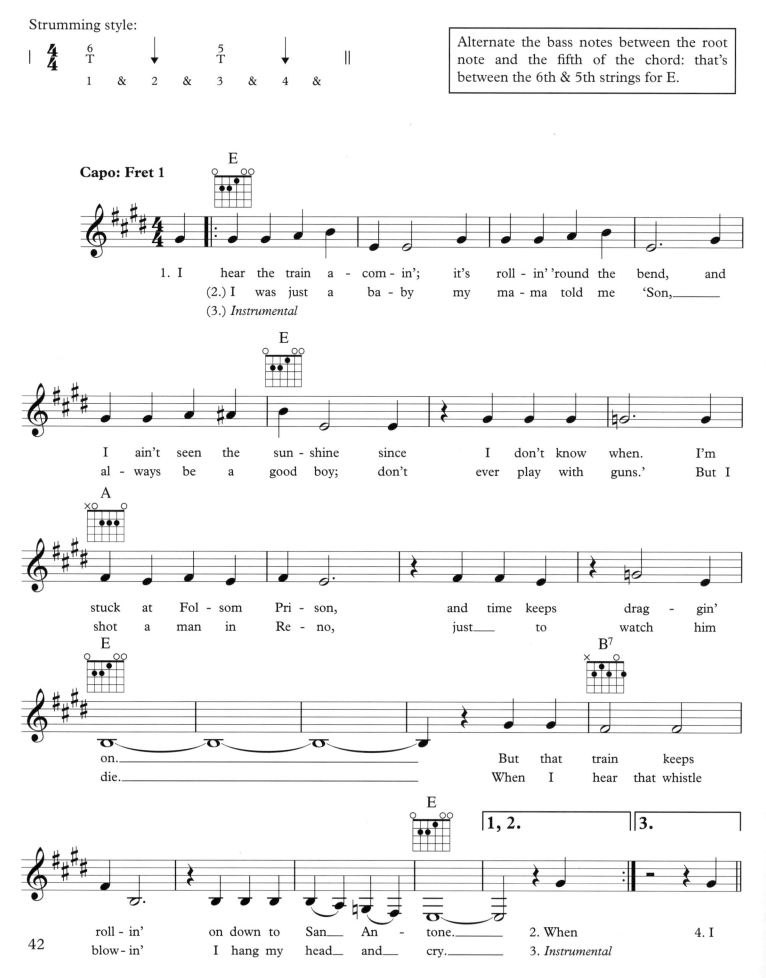

1. I hear the train a-comin'; it's rollin' 'round the bend, and
(2.) I was just a ba-by my ma-ma told me 'Son,___
(3.) Instrumental

I ain't seen the sun-shine since I don't know when. I'm
al-ways be a good boy; don't ever play with guns.' But I

stuck at Fol-som Pri-son, and time keeps drag-gin'
shot a man in Re-no, just___ to watch him

on.___
die.___

But that train keeps
When I hear that whistle

1, 2.   **3.**

roll-in' on down to San___ An-tone.___ 2. When
blow-in' I hang my head___ and___ cry.___ 3. Instrumental

42

Friday I'm In Love

Words by Robert Smith
Music by Robert Smith, Simon Gallup, Perry Bamonte, Porl Thompson & Boris Williams

Strumming style:

Capo: Fret 1

Verse

1, 5. I don't care___ if Mon - day's blue,___
2, 6. Mon - day you can fall___ a - part,
3. I don't care___ if Mon - day's black,___
4. Mon - day you can hold___ your head,___

Tues-day's grey___ and Wednes - day too.___ Thurs - day I don't care___
Tues - day, Wednes-day break___ my heart._ Oh, Thurs - day does n't ev -
Tues - day, Wednes-day heart___ at - tack.___ Thurs - day nev - er look -
Tues - day, Wednes-day stay___ in bed.___ Or Thurs - day watch the walls___

Fine

___ a - bout___ you,___ it's Fri - day, I'm in love.___
- en start,___ it's Fri - day, I'm in love.___ *(2. To Chorus)*
- ing back,___ it's Fri - day, I'm in love.___
___ in - stead,___ it's Fri - day I'm in love.___ *(4. To Chorus)*

Chorus

Sat - ur - day___ wait, 'cause Sun - day al - ways comes___

44

Fifty Ways To Leave Your Lover

Words & Music by Paul Simon

Play sparsely-picked chords in the verse, before switching to a choppy up-tempo strumming style in the chorus.

Hallelujah

Words & Music by Leonard Cohen

Arpeggio style:

Focus on playing the picking pattern as precisely as possible. Let the notes of the chord ring out—this will really help the music flow.

Capo: Fret 5

(1.) heard there was a se-cret chord that Da-vid played and it pleased the Lord, but
(2.) faith was strong but you need-ed proof. You saw her bath-ing on the roof, her

(Verse 3, 4 & 6 see block lyrics)

(Verse 5 Instrumental)

you don't real-ly care for mu-sic do ya? Well, it
beau-ty and the moon-light ov-er-threw ya. And she

Verse 3:
Well, baby I've been here before
I've seen this room, and I've walked this floor,
You know, I used to live alone before I knew you.
And I've seen your flag on the marble arch
And love is not a victory march,
It's a cold and it's a broken Hallelujah.

Verse 4:
Well, there was a time when you let me know
What's really going on below,
But now you never show that to me do ya?
But remember when I moved in you
And the holy dove was moving too,
And every breath we drew was Hallelujah.

Verse 6:
Maybe there's a God above,
But all I've ever learned from love
Was how to shoot somebody who outdrew ya.
And it's not a cry that you hear at night,
It's not somebody who's seen the light,
It's a cold and it's a broken Hallelujah.

Hey, Soul Sister

Words & Music by Espen Lind, Pat Monahan & Amund Bjorklund

53

need. So gang-ster, I'm__ so thug._ You're the on-ly one__ I'm dream-ing of.__ You see

I can be my-self__ now fi-nal-ly. In fact__there's noth-ing I__ can't be.__

D.S. al Coda

__ I want the world to see__ you be-ing with__ me.__

Coda

thing you do__ to - night.__ Hey soul sis-ter, I__don't wan-na miss a sin-gle

thing you do_____ to-night.__ Hey,__ hey,__

1.

__ hey._____ to-night.__ __

2.

to-night.__

Ho Hey

Words & Music by Jeremy Fraites & Wesley Schultz

Chorus

(Hey! Two, three...) I be-long with you, you be-long with me you're my___ sweet-

- heart.___ I be-long with you, you be-long with me you're my___ sweet...

D.S. al Coda

Ho! Hey! Ho! Hey!

Coda

(Hey!) (Ho!) And she'd be stand-ing next___ to me._____

Chorus

(Hey! Two, three...) I be-long with you, you be-long with me you're my___ sweet-

Imagine

Words & Music by John Lennon

Arpeggio style:

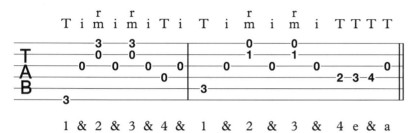

The picking shown here is specific to the intro and verse, which alternate between G and C. Try simple strumming for the chorus.

Capo: Fret 5

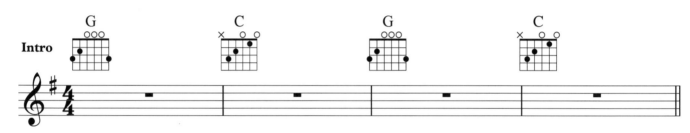

1. I - ma - gine there's no hea - ven,____
2. I - ma - gine there's no coun - tries,____
3. I - ma - gine no po - ses - sions,____

it's ea - sy if you try.____
it is - n't hard to do.____
I won - der if you can.____

No hell____ be - low us,____
No - thing to kill or die for,
No need for greed or hun - ger,

59

Homeward Bound

Words & Music by Paul Simon

The strumming for this song is extremely simple, so it needs to be accurate to provide a rock-solid beat and convincing feel.

Capo: Fret 3

home - ward_____ bound.

Home, where my thought's____ es - ca - ping,

home, where my mu - sic's play - ing,

home, where my love_____ lies wait - ing si - lent - ly

1, 2.

for me._____

3. To -

3.

Si - lent - ly for me._____

I Will Wait

Words & Music by Mumford & Sons

Strumming style:

1 e & a 2 e & a 3 e & a 4 e & a

Capo: Fret 1

Intro — Am, G/B, C, F(add9), C/E, G

Verse — C, F

1. And I came home_ like a stone and I fell
   dust_ which we've known will blow a-

C, G(sus4)

heav - y in - to your arms. These days of But
- way____ with this new sun.

[1.] These days of

[2.] But

Pre-chorus — Am, G/B, C, F(add9), C/E, G

I'll____ kneel down, wait for now.____ And
I'll____ kneel down, know my ground.____

Chorus C, Em, G(sus4)

I will_ wait, I will_ wait for you. And

63

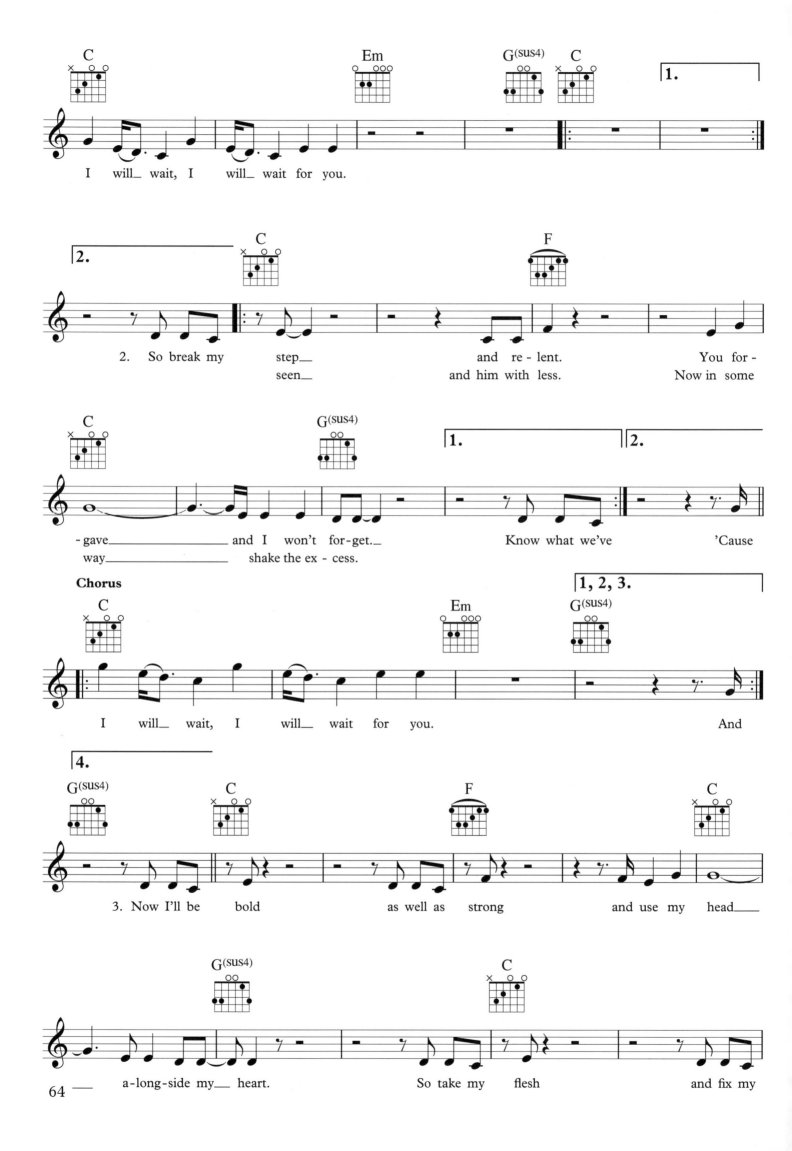

eyes,   a teth-ered mind_____ free from the_ lies.

Bridge

I'll_____ kneel down, wait for   now._____
I'll_____ kneel down, know my

1.

2.   **Instrumental**

ground._____

Raise_____ my_____ hands,_
bow_____ my_____ head,_

1.   **2.**   **Chorus**

paint my spi - rit gold._____ And
keep my heart_   slow._____   'Cause

Play 4 times

I will_ wait, I will_ wait for you.   (And)

The Joker

Words & Music by Steve Miller, Eddie Curtis & Ahmet Ertegun

The album version of this song is longer—and in a different key! This arrangement matches the single version.

Riff:

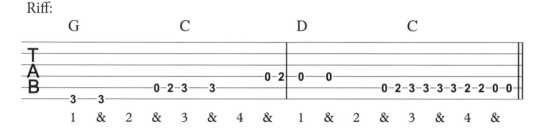

To match recording, tune down one semitone

Verse

1. Some peo-ple call me the space cow-boy.   Yeah!__

(Verse 2: 8 bars instrumental)

3.   Peo-ple keep talk ing a-bout me baby,

Some call me the gang-ster of love.__   Some peo-ple call me Mau-rice,

say I'm do-in' you wrong.__   But don't you wor-ry, don't wor-

__   cos I speak   of the Pom-pa-tus of   love.__

- ry, no, don't wor-ry, Ma-ma,   cos   I'm right here   at   home.

(1.) Peo-ple talk a-bout me ba-by;   Say I'm do-in' you wrong, do-in' you

(2, 3.) You're the cu-test thing that I ev-er did see,   I love your peach - es, want to

(3° fade begins)

Knockin' On Heaven's Door

Words & Music by Bob Dylan

Strumming style:

Keep the strumming hand moving in sixteenth-notes throughout, but play simple eighth-notes on beats 1 and 3.

Verse

1. Ma - ma, take__ this badge_ from me.____

(Verse 2 see block lyrics)

I can't use it a - ny - more.____

It's get - ting dark,____ too dark__ to see;____

I feel like I'm knock - in' on hea - ven's door.____

Chorus

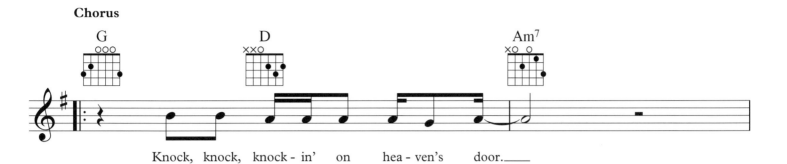

Knock, knock, knock - in' on hea - ven's door.____

D.C. al Coda
To Coda ⊕

Knock, knock, knock - in' on hea - ven's door.____

⊕ *Coda*

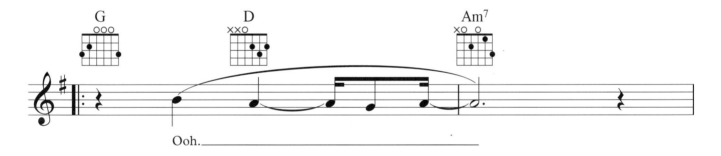

Ooh.____

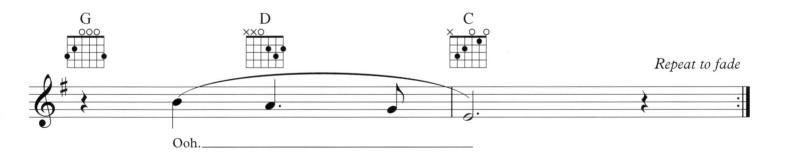

Repeat to fade

Ooh.____

Verse 2:
Mama, put my guns in the ground
I can't shoot them anymore
That long black cloud is comin' down
I feel like I'm knockin' on Heaven's door.

Jolene

Words & Music by Dolly Parton

Arpeggio style:

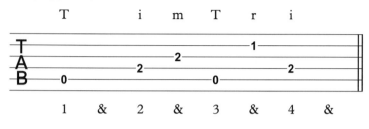

> Practise the picking pattern on the A minor chord several times before trying it with the other chords.

Capo: Fret 4

Intro

Chorus

- lene, Jo - lene, Jo - lene, Jo - lene,____

____ I'm beg - ging of___ you; please___ don't_ take my___ man.___

Jo - lene, Jo -

lene, Jo - lene, Jo - lene,____

To Coda ⊕

71

Lay, Lady, Lay

Words & Music by Bob Dylan

Strumming style:

1 e & a 2 e & a 3 e & a 4 e & a

Intro A C#m G Bm

Chorus A C#m G Bm

Lay, la - dy, lay,___ lay a - cross my big brass bed.
Lay, la - dy, lay,___ lay a - cross my big brass bed.___

Verse A C#m G Bm E F#m

What - ev - er col - ors you have___

A E F#m A

in your mind,___ I'll show them to you and you'll see them shine.

Why wait an-y long-er for___ the one you love,___ when he's stand-

-ing in front of you.___

Chorus

Lay, la-dy, lay,___
Stay, la-dy, stay,___

lay a-cross my big brass bed.___
stay while the night___ is still a-head.___

Verse

I long___ to see___ you in the morn-ing light,___ I long to reach for you

in the night. **Chorus** Stay, la-dy, stay,___ stay while the night___ is still a-head.__

Let It Be

Words & Music by John Lennon & Paul McCartney

The fast-changing chord sequences emulate the original piano part. Simplify these by only playing the chords that occur on strong beats if you like.

Verse 2:
And when the broken hearted people living in the world agree,
There will be an answer, let it be.
For though they may be parted, there is still a chance that they might see,
There will be an answer, let it be.

Let it be...

Verse 3:
And when the night is cloudy there is still a light that shines on me,
Shine until tomorrow, let it be.
I wake up to the sound of music, Mother Mary comes to me,
Speaking words of wisdom, let it be.

Life On Mars?

Words & Music by David Bowie

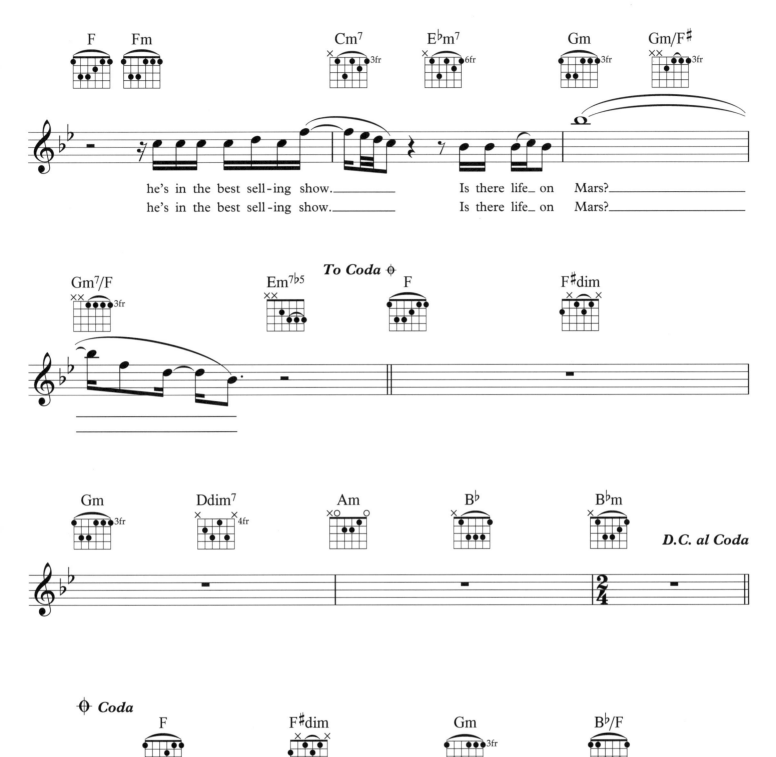

he's in the best sell-ing show._____   Is there life_ on   Mars?_____

he's in the best sell-ing show._____   Is there life_ on   Mars?_____

To Coda ⊕

D.C. al Coda

⊕ ***Coda***

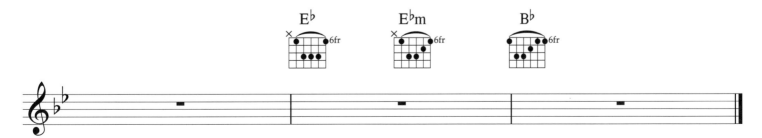

Love Story

Words & Music by Taylor Swift

Make You Feel My Love

Words & Music by Bob Dylan

Mrs. Robinson

Words & Music by Paul Simon

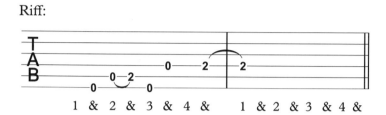

You can play the picked riff wherever you see the chord of **E**, or else use the strumming pattern throughout.

De de de de de de de de de de de de._____

Do do do do do do do do do._____

De de de de de de de de de_____ de de de de de._____

And here's to you__

Ordinary World

Words & Music by John Taylor, Nick Rhodes, Simon Le Bon & Warren Cuccurullo

Strumming style:

Capo: Fret 4

Lyrics:

1. Came in from a rai - ny Thurs - day on the av - e - nue,___
2. Pas - sion or co - in - ci - dence_ once prompt - ed you to say,___
3. Pa - pers in the road - side tell___ of suf - fer - ing and greed,___

thought I heard you talk - ing soft - ly.   I turned on the lights, the T. - V.
'Pride will tear us both a - part.'___   Well, now pride's gone out the win - dow cross the
here to - day, for got___ to mor - row,   Ooh,___ here be - sides the news of ho - ly

To Coda ⊕

and the rad - i - o,___   still I can't es - cape_ the ghost of___ you.___
roof - top run a - way,___   left me in the vac - uum of___ my - heart.
war and ho - ly need,___   ours is just a lit - tle sor - rowed_ talk.___

Guitar Solo

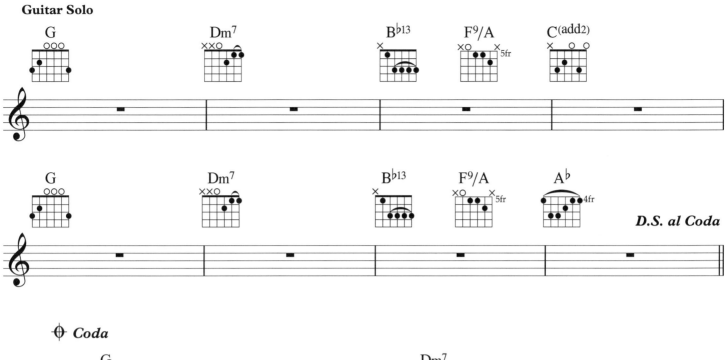

D.S. al Coda

✦ *Coda*

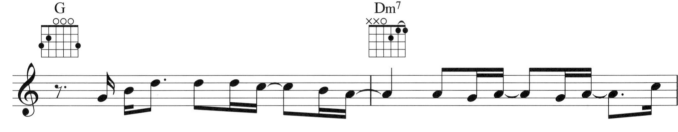

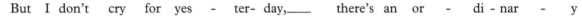

But I don't cry for yes - ter - day,___ there's an or - di - nar - y

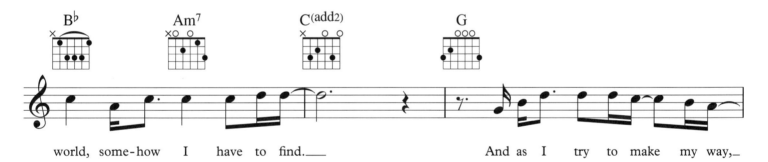

world, some-how I have to find.___ And as I try to make my way,___

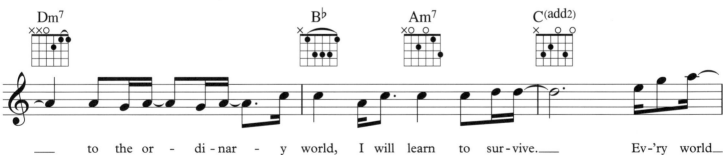

___ to the or - di - nar - y world, I will learn to sur - vive.___ Ev-'ry world___

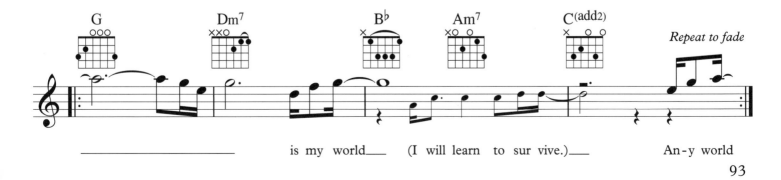

Repeat to fade

_____ is my world___ (I will learn to sur vive.)___ An-y world

Redemption Song

Words & Music by Bob Marley

Strumming style:

Strum in even eighth-notes, accenting the first strum of each beat and 'ghosting' the others—then experiment with accents for some lively alterations.

1. Old pi - rates, yes they rob I. Sold_ I to the mer-chant ships.
(2,3.) -pate your-selves from men-tal slav-'ry; none but our - selves can free our minds._

_ Have no fear for a - to-mic e-ner-gy, 'cause none of them can stop the time._
_ min-utes af-ter they_took I from the bot-tom-less

_ pit. But my hand_ was made_ strong by the hand of the Al - might -
_ How long shall they kill our pro-phets while we stand a - side and look?_

- y. We for - ward in this ge - ne - ra - tion_ tri - um - phant -
_ Some say_ it's just a part of it. We've got to ful - fill the_

Rocket Man

Words & Music by Elton John & Bernie Taupin

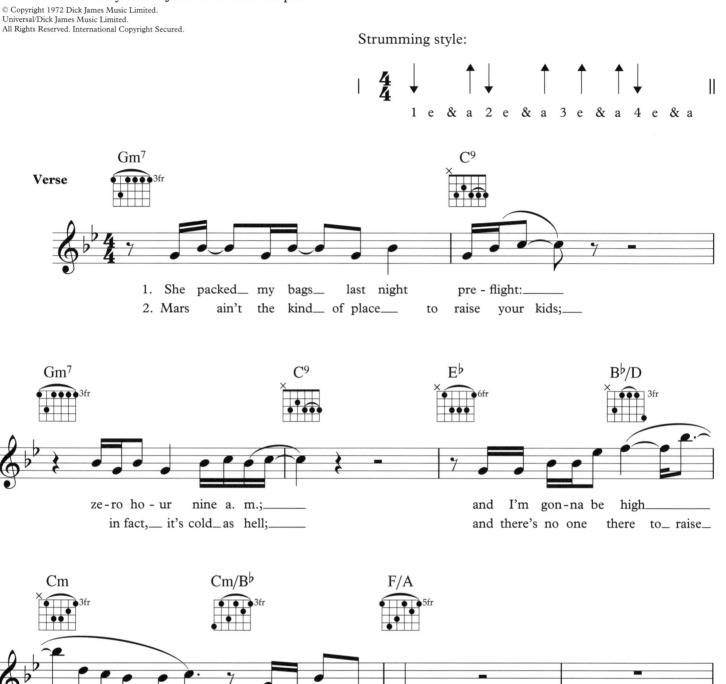

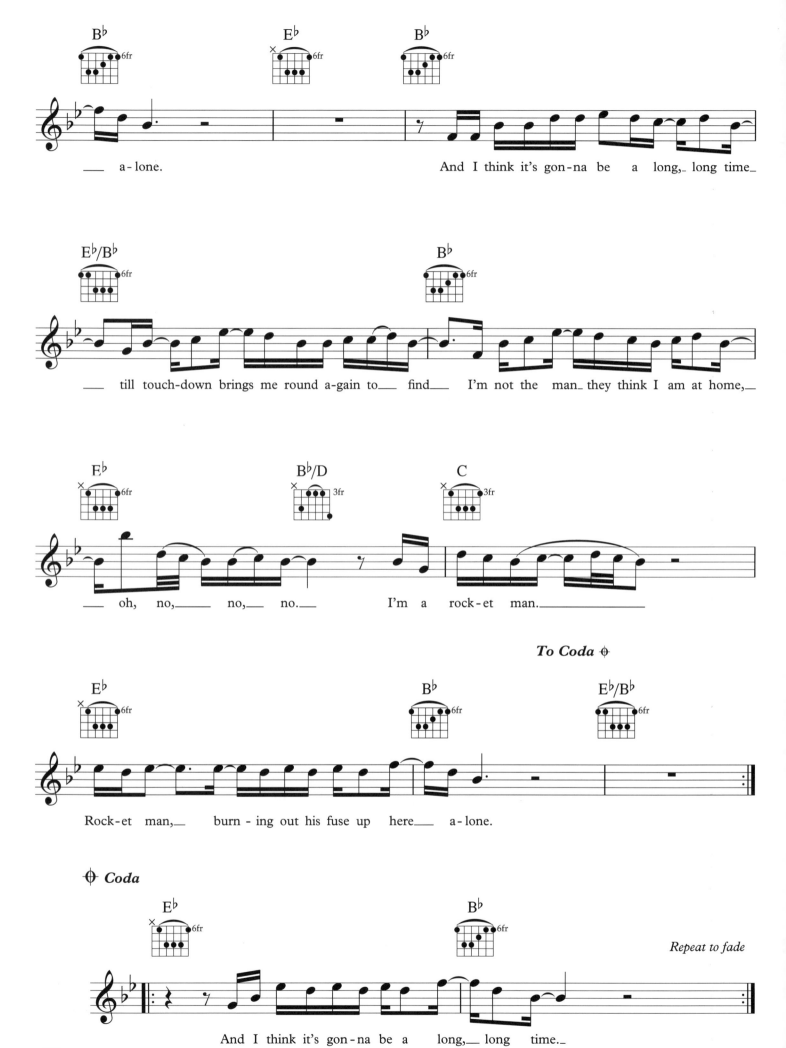

_____ a-lone.

And I think it's gon-na be a long,_ long time_

_____ till touch-down brings me round a-gain to_ find_ I'm not the man_ they think I am at home,_

_____ oh, no,_____ no,_ no._ I'm a rock-et man._____

To Coda ⊕

Rock-et man,_ burn-ing out his fuse up here_ a-lone.

⊕ **Coda**

Repeat to fade

And I think it's gon-na be a long,_ long time._

Romeo And Juliet

Words & Music by Mark Knopfler

Capo: Fret 3

Intro

Verse

1, 4. A love-struck Ro - me - o

(*Verses 2 & 3, see block lyrics*)

sings a street-suss se - re - nade,___

lay-ing ev -'ry - bo - dy low___ with a love song that___ he made,___

finds___ a street-light, steps out of the shade, says some-thing like,

'You and me babe,___ how a - bout it?'___

Verse 4 **Fine**

Ju - li - et says, 'Hey, it's Ro - me - o, you near - ly gim - me a heart at - tack.'

He's un - der - neath the win - dow, she's sing - ing 'Hey la, my boy - friend's back,

you should - n't come a - round here, sing - ing up at peo - ple like that,

An - y - way, what you gon - na do a - bout___ it?'_____ Ju - li -

Chorus

- et, the dice were load - ed from___ the start,___ and I

(Chorus 2 & 3, see block lyrics)

100 bet, and you ex - plod - ed in - to my heart and I for -

-get, I___ for - get   the mov - ie song.

When__ you gon-na re - a - lise   it was just that the time was wrong,

D.S. al Fine

(3° play Link x 2)

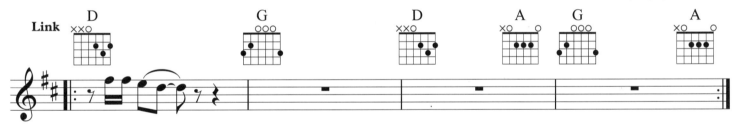

Ju - li - et?___

Verse 2:
Come up on different streets
They both were streets of shame
Both dirty, both mean
Yes, and the dream was just the same
And I dreamed your dream for you
And now your dream is real
How can you look at me as if I was
Just another one of your deals?

Where you can fall for chains of silver
You can fall for chains of gold
You can fall for pretty strangers
And the promises they hold
You promised me everything
You promised me thick and thin, yeah
Now you just say 'Oh Romeo, yeah,
You know I used to have a scene with him'.

Chorus 2:
Juliet, when we made love you used to cry
You said, 'I love you like the stars above,
I'll love you till I die.'
There's a place for us, you know the movie song
When you gonna realise
It was just that the time was wrong, Juliet?

Verse 3:
I can't do the talk
Like they talk on the T.V.
And I can't do a love song
Like the way it's meant to be
I can't do everything
But I'd do anything for you
I can't do anything
Except be in love with you.

And all I do is miss you
And the way we used to be
All I do is keep the beat
And bad company
All I do is kiss you
Through the bars of a rhyme
Julie, I'd do the stars with you
Any time.

Chorus 3:
Juliet, when we made love you used to cry
You said, 'I love you like the stars above,
I'll love you till I die.'
There's a place for us, you know the movie song
When you gonna realise
It was just that the time was wrong, Juliet?

101

Save Tonight

Words & Music by Eagle-Eye Cherry

Strum in even eighth-notes, adding ghosted sixteenth-note strums where shown. This will create a more delicate and dynamic strumming rhythm.

Strumming style:

The Scientist

Words & Music by Guy Berryman, Chris Martin, Jon Buckland & Will Champion

Strumming style:

The strumming style for this song uses steady eighth-note strumming, with the on-beat strums accented—and all played with a down strum.

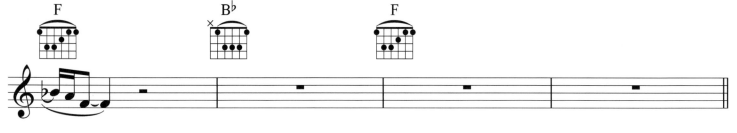

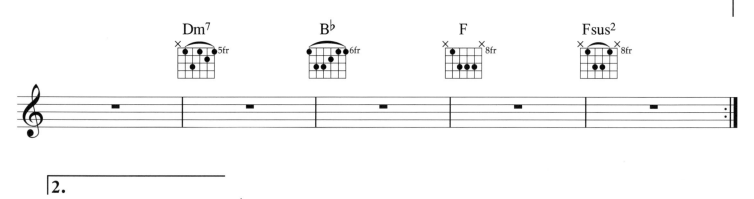

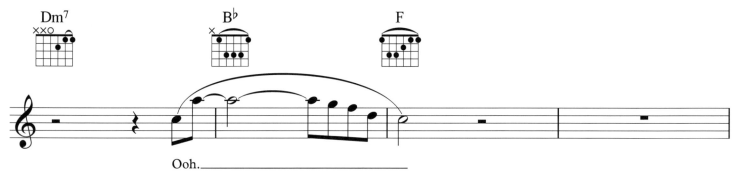

Ooh._____

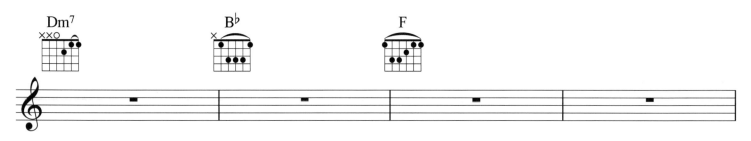

Ah,   ooh._____

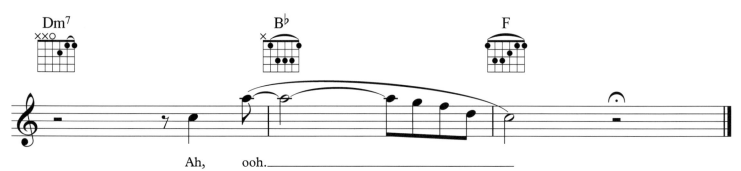

Ah,   ooh._____

Sing

Words & Music by Fran Healy

Arpeggio style:

Strum simple eighth-notes, or else try this picking pattern, which emulates the original banjo part.

Capo: Fret 2

1. Ba - by, you've been go - in' so cra - zy, late - ly no - thin' seems to be go - in' right. So_ a - lone, oh, why d'ya have_ to get so_ a - lone? You're_ sore you've been wait - in' in the sun too_ long._ But if you sing,_

2. Cold - er, cry - ing ov - er your shoul - der, hold_ her, tell her ev - 'ry - thing's gon - na be fine. Sure - ly you've been go - ing_ to hur - ry. Hur - ry, 'cause no - one's_ gon - na be stopped. Not if you sing,

Chorus

Space Oddity

Words & Music by David Bowie

Interlude

God's love be with you.
Lift off!

(Space craft lift-off effects)

Chorus

This is ground con - trol__ to Ma - jor Tom,__ you've real - ly made the grade!__
This is Ma - jor Tom__ to ground con - trol,____ I'm step - ping through the door,__

And the pa - pers want to know__ whose shirts you wear,
And I'm float - ing in a most__ pe - cu - liar way,__

Now it's time to leave the cap - sule if you dare.__
And the stars look ve - ry dif - fe - rent to - day.__

(2°)
(For) here am I
Here am I

sit - ting in a tin can____ far_____ a - bove__ the world.____
float - ing round my tin can____ far_____ a - bove__ the moon.____

Pla - net Earth__ is blue and there's no - thing I can do.
Pla - net Earth__ is blue and there's no - thing I can do.

Bridge

Guitar solo

(ad lib.)

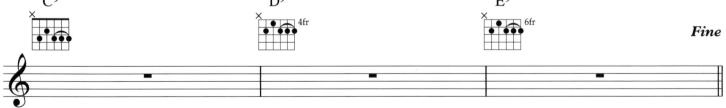

Fine

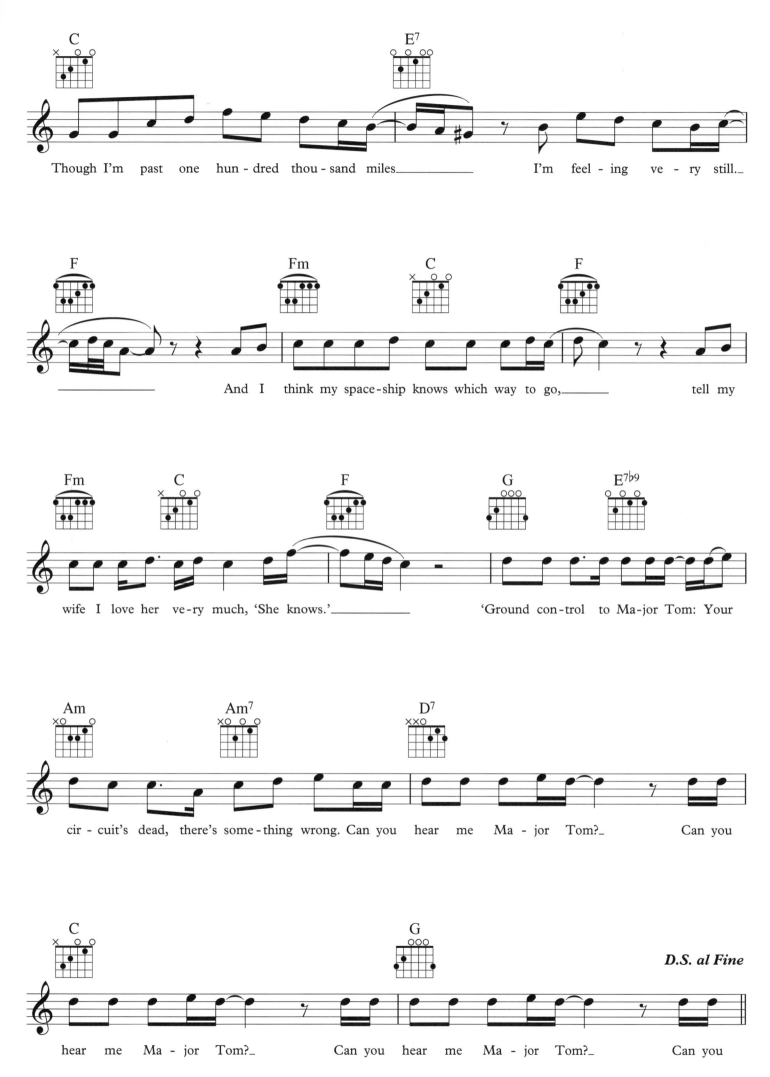

Stand By Me

Words & Music by Ben E. King, Jerry Leiber & Mike Stoller

Strumming style:

Create a percussive 'slap' on beats 2 and 4 by bringing the strumming hand down hard onto the strings, providing a backbeat.

Capo: Fret 2

Verse

G

1. When the night_____ has come_____
(2.) _____ that we look up - on

Em   D   Em   C

and the land is___ dark,_____ and the moon_____ is the on -
should tum-ble and___ fall, or the moun - tain should

D   G

- ly_____ light___ we'll see. No, I won't___
crum - ble_____ to_____ the sea. I won't cry,___

be a - fraid;_____ no, I
I won't cry;_____ no, I won't

Chorus

115

The Sound Of Silence

Words & Music by Paul Simon

Picking style:

Capo: Fret 1

1. Hel - lo dark - ness, my old friend.
2. In rest - less dreams I walked a - lone
3. And in the nak - ed light I saw
4. 'Fools!' said I, 'You do not know

I've come to talk with you a - gain,
nar - row streets of cob - ble - stone,
ten thou - sand peo - ple, may - be more.
si - lence like a can - cer grows.'

be - cause a vi - sion soft - ly creep - ing,   left its seeds while I was
'neath the ha - lo of a street lamp,   I turned my col - lar to the
Peo - ple talk - ing with - out speak - ing,   peo - ple hear - ing with - out
'Hear my words that I might teach you,   take my arms that I might

sleep - ing, and the vi - sion_____ that was
cold and damp_ when my eyes were stabbed by the
lis - ten - ing_ peo - ple writ - ing songs_____ that_____
reach you'_ but my words like_____

1-3.

plant - ed in my brain still re - mains
flash of a ne - on light that split the night
voi - ces_ nev - er share and no one dare
si - lent rain - drops

with - in the sound of si - lence._____
and touched the sound of si - lence._____
dis - turb the sound of si - lence._____

4.

fell, and ech - oed_____ in the

wells of si - lence._____ 5. And the peo - ple bowed and

117

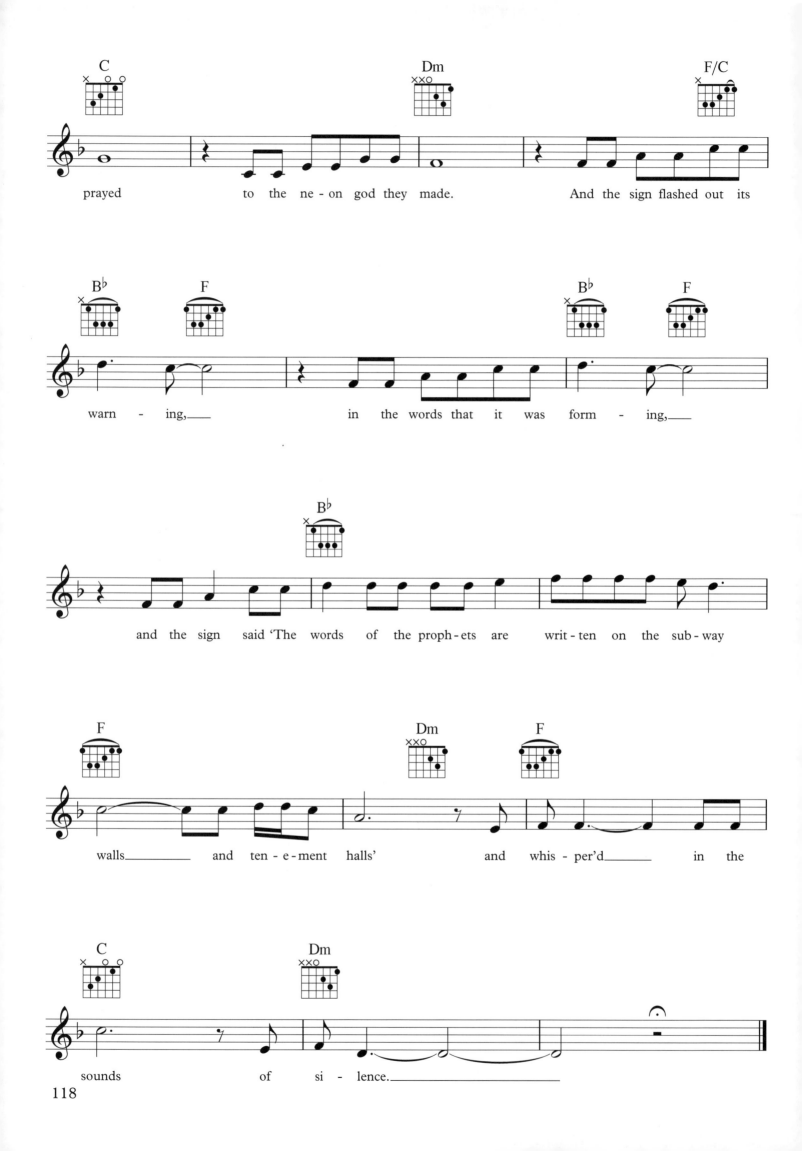

prayed to the ne - on god they made. And the sign flashed out its

warn - ing,___ in the words that it was form - ing,___

and the sign said 'The words of the proph - ets are writ - ten on the sub - way

walls___ and ten - e - ment halls' and whis - per'd___ in the

sounds of si - lence.___

Tears In Heaven

Words & Music by Eric Clapton & Will Jennings

Picking style:

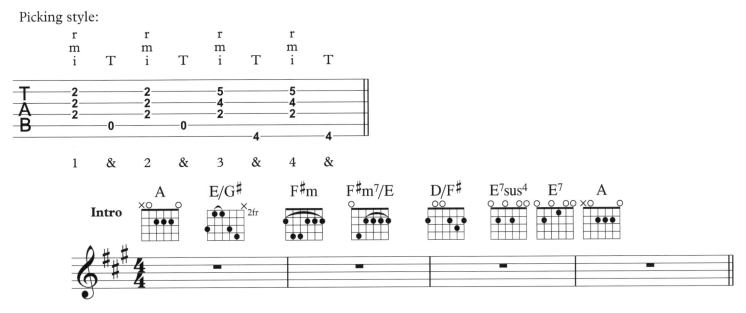

(1.3.) Would you know my name_____ if I saw you in heav-

(2.) Would you hold my hand_____ if I saw you in heav-

- en? Would it be the same___

- en? Would you help me stand___

if I saw you in heav - en?

if I saw you in heav - en?

Chorus

(1,4.) I must be strong____ and car - ry on____
(2.) I'll find my way____ through night and day____
(3.) Be - yond the door____ there's peace I'm sure,

Verse 4 to Coda

____ 'cause I know____ I don't be - long____ here in heav -
____ 'cause I know____ I just can't stay____ here in heav -
____ and I know____ there'll be no more____ tears in heav -

1, 3.

- en.
- en.
- en.

2.

Bridge

Time can bring you down____ time can bend your knees.____

Time can break your heart,____

120

have you beg- gin' please___ beg- gin' please.___

D.S. al Coda

Coda

en. 'Cause I know I don't be-long___ here in heav -

- en.

121

Torn

Words & Music by Anne Preven, Phil Thornalley & Scott Cutler

Verse 2:
So I guess the fortune-teller's right,
I should have seen just what was there
And not some holy light.
But you crawled beneath my veins
And now I don't care I had no luck,
I don't miss it all that much.
There's just so many things
That I can't touch, I'm torn.

Verse 3:
There's nothing where he used to lie,
My inspiration has all run dry,
That's what's going on,
Nothing's right, I'm torn.

Vincent (Starry Starry Night)

Words & Music by Don McLean

Picking style:

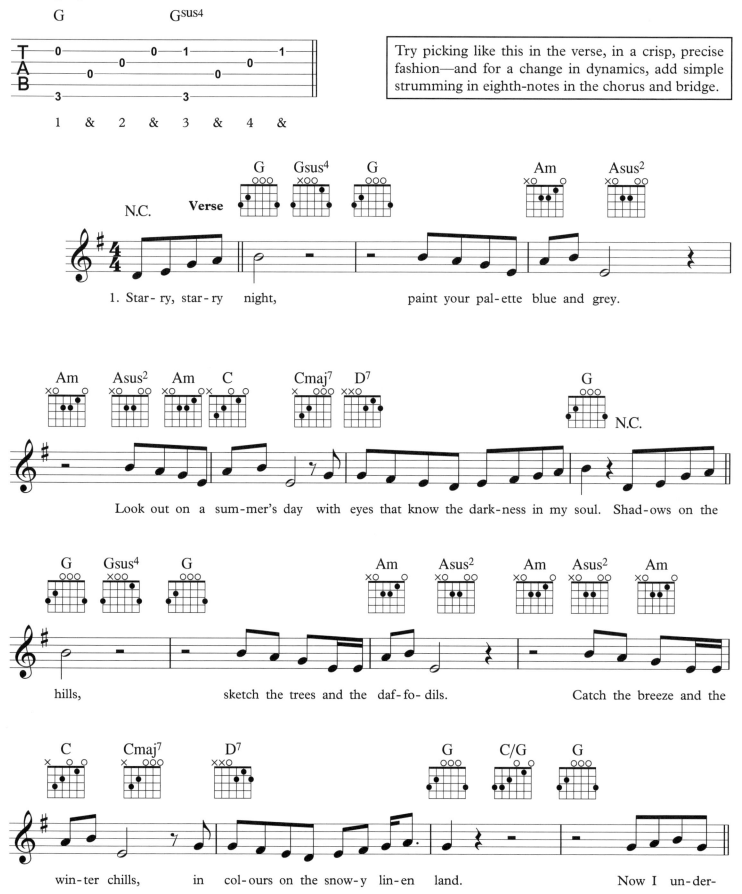

Try picking like this in the verse, in a crisp, precise fashion—and for a change in dynamics, add simple strumming in eighth-notes in the chorus and bridge.

1. Star-ry, star-ry night, paint your pal-ette blue and grey.

Look out on a sum-mer's day with eyes that know the dark-ness in my soul. Shad-ows on the

hills, sketch the trees and the daf-fo-dils. Catch the breeze and the

win-ter chills, in col-ours on the snow-y lin-en land. Now I un-der-

Chorus

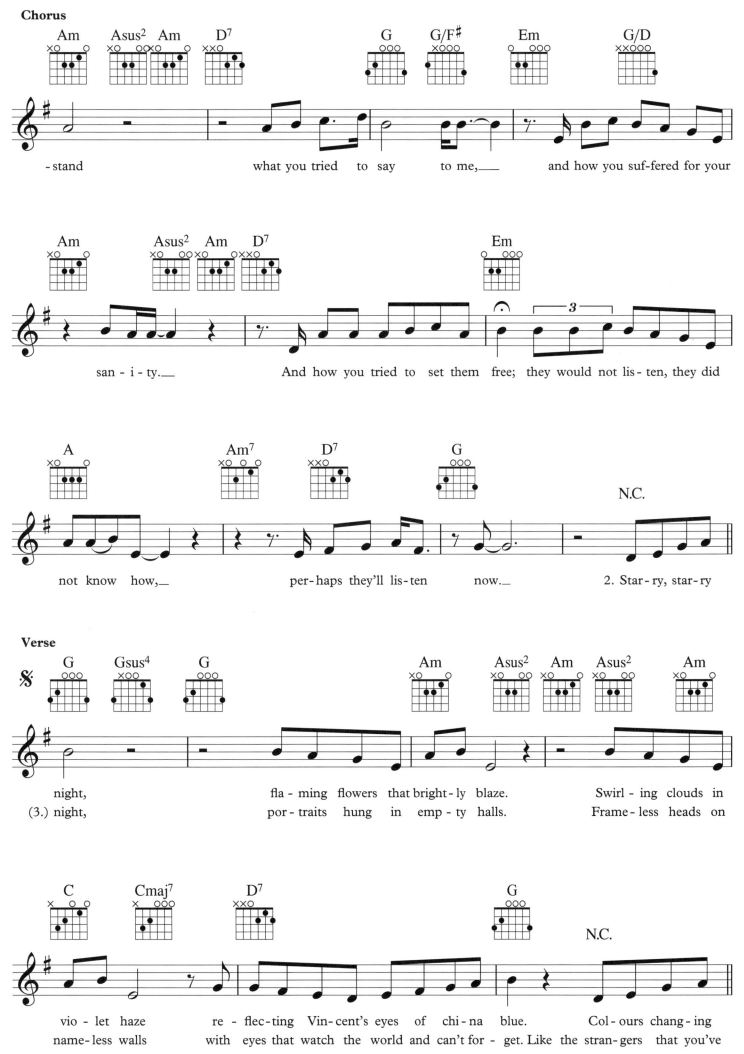

- stand   what you tried   to say   to me,___   and how you suf-fered for your

san - i - ty.___   And how you tried to   set them   free;   they would not lis - ten, they did

not know   how,___   per-haps they'll lis-ten   now.___   2. Star - ry, star - ry

Verse

night,   fla - ming flowers that bright - ly blaze.   Swirl - ing clouds in
(3.) night,   por - traits hung   in emp - ty halls.   Frame - less heads on

vio - let haze   re - flec - ting Vin - cent's eyes of chi - na blue.   Col - ours chang - ing
name - less walls   with eyes that watch the world and can't for - get. Like the stran - gers   that you've

hue,   mor-ning fields of am-ber grain.   Weath-ered fa-ces

met,   the rag-ged men in rag-ged clothes.   a sil - ver thorn of

lined in pain___ are soothed be-neath the art-ist's___ lov-ing hand. Now I un-der-

blood-y rose,___ lie crushed and bro-ken on the___ vir-gin snow. Now I think I

Chorus

- stand   what you tried to say to me, and how you suf-fered for___ your

know   what you tried to say to me, and how you suf-fered for___ your

To Coda ⊕

san - i - ty.___ And how you tried to set them free; they would not lis-ten, they did

san - i - ty.___ And how you tried to set them

not know___ how,___ per-haps they'll lis-ten now. For they could not___

126

Bridge

love you,— but still your love was true.—

And when no hope was left in sight,— on that star-ry, star-ry night, you

took your life as lov-ers of-ten do. But I could have told you Vin-cent, this

D.S. al Coda

world was nev-er meant for one as beau-ti-ful— as you. 3. Star-ry star-ry

Coda

free; they would not lis-ten, they're not list-'ning still.— Per-haps they nev-er

will.— *(Guitar)*

The Weight

Words & Music by Robbie Robertson (The Band)

Strumming style:

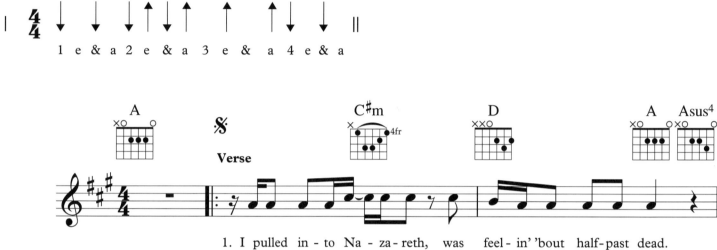

Verse

1. I pulled in - to Na - za - reth, was feel - in' 'bout half-past dead.
2. I picked up my__ bag, I went look - ing for a place to hide,
3. Go down, Miss Mos - es, there's no - thing you can say,

I just need some place__ where I can lay__ my head.__
when I saw Car - men and the De - vil walk - ing side by side.__
it's just ol'__ Luke, and Luke's wait - ing on the judge - ment day.__

'Hey, mis - ter can you tell me__ where a man might find a bed?'__
I said, 'Hey, Car - men,__ come on, let's go down - town.'
'Well, Luke, my friend,__ what a - bout young An - na Lee?'__

He just grinned and shook my hand,___ 'No' was all___ he said.
She said,___ 'I got - ta go, but my friend can stick a round.
He said, 'Do me a fa - vour son,___ won't you stay and keep An - na Lee com - pa - ny?'

Chorus

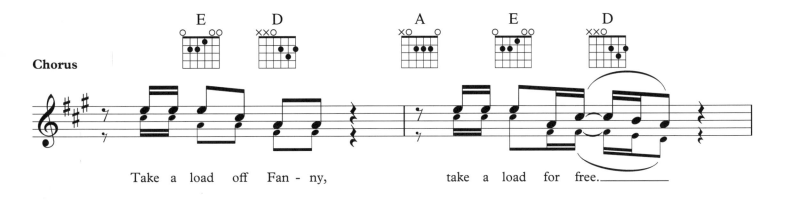

Take a load off Fan - ny,   take a load for free.___

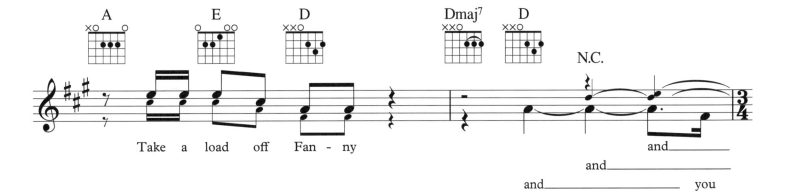

Take a load off Fan - ny

and___
and___
and___ you

1-3.

To Coda ⊕

___ you put the load right on me.___
put the load right on me.

Verse 4
Crazy Chester followed me and he caught me in the fog.
He said, 'I will fix your rack if you take Jack, my dog.'
I said, 'Wait a minute, Chester, you know, I'm a peaceful man.'
He said, 'That's okay boy, won't you feed him when you can?'

Take a load off, Fanny etc.

Verse 5
Catch a cannonball, now, to take me down the line.
My bag is sinking low and I do believe it's time
To get back to Miss Fanny, you know, she's the only one
Who sent me here with her regards for everyone.

Take a load off, Fanny etc.

Wild World

Words & Music by Cat Stevens

Strumming style:

Strum two accented eighth-notes followed by a group of four sixteenth-notes, as shown, for a flowing feel to the rhythm.

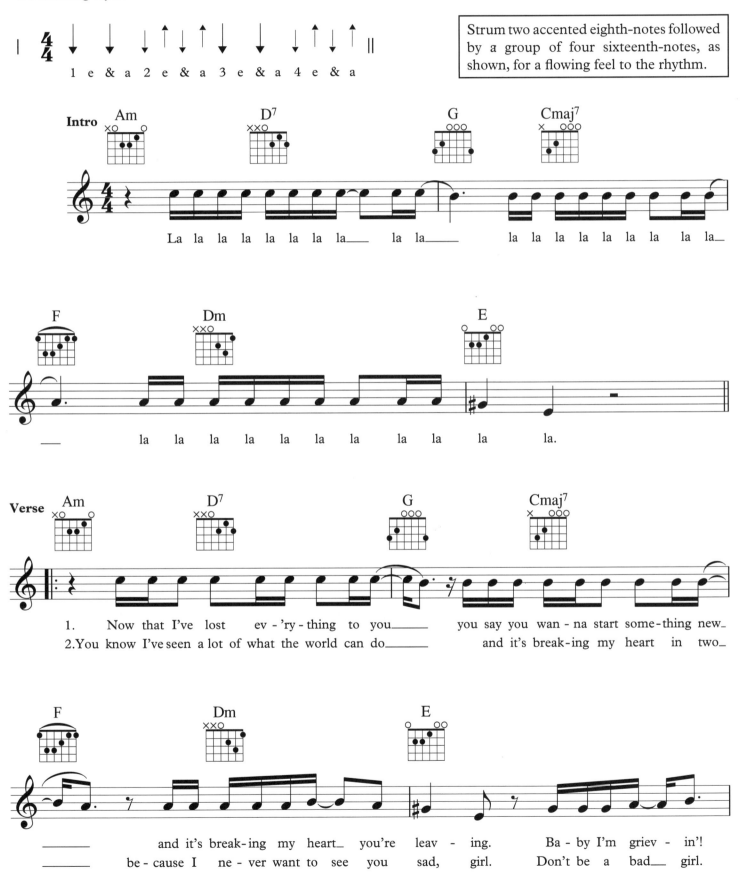

La la la la la la la la___ la la___ la la la la la la la la___

___ la la la la la la la la la la la la.

Verse

1. Now that I've lost ev-'ry-thing to you___ you say you wan-na start some-thing new_
2. You know I've seen a lot of what the world can do___ and it's break-ing my heart in two_

___ and it's break-ing my heart_ you're leav-ing. Ba-by I'm griev-in'!
___ be-cause I ne-ver want to see you sad, girl. Don't be a bad_ girl.

But if you want to leave take good care, hope you have a lot of nice things to wear___
But if you want to leave take good care, hope you make a lot of nice friends out there___

___ but then a lot of nice things turn bad out there___
___ but just re-mem-ber there's a lot of bad and be - ware___

Chorus

Oh ba - by, ba - by it's a

wild world. It's hard to get by___ just up - on a

smile. Oh, ba - by, ba - by it's a wild world.

I'll al-ways re-mem-ber you___ like a child, girl.___

Ba-by I love___ you, but if you want to leave___ take good

care, hope you make a lot of nice friends out there. But just re-mem-ber there's a lot of bad

D.S. al Coda
(repeat chorus)

and be-ware.___

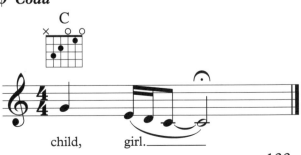

♦ *Coda*

child, girl.___

Wonderwall

Words & Music by Noel Gallagher

Strumming style:

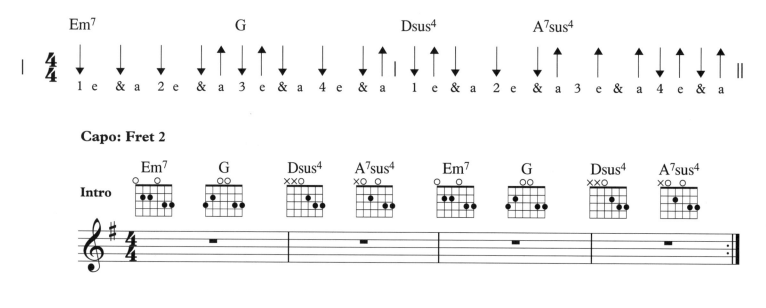

Capo: Fret 2

Intro

Verse

1. To - day   is gon - na be the day that they're gon-na throw it back to you.—
2. Back-beat   the word was on the street that the fi - re in your heart is out.—
3. To - day   was gon - na be the day but they'll nev - er throw it back to you.—

By now   you should-'ve some-how re - al - ised   what you got - ta do.—⎫
I'm sure you've heard it   all before but you nev - er real - ly had a doubt.⎬
By now   you should-'ve some-how re - al - ised   what you're not to do.—⎭

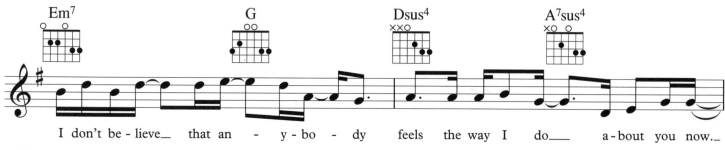

I don't be - lieve— that an - y - bo - dy feels the way I do— a-bout you now.—

You're Still The One

Words & Music by Shania Twain & R.J. Lange

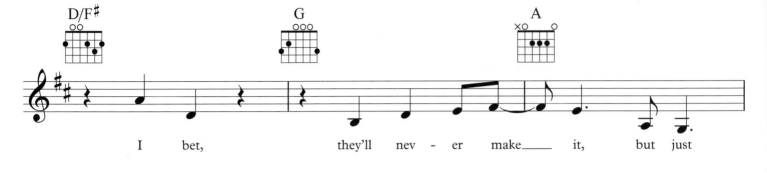

I bet, they'll nev - er make___ it, but just

look at___ us hold - ing___ on,___ we're still to - geth -

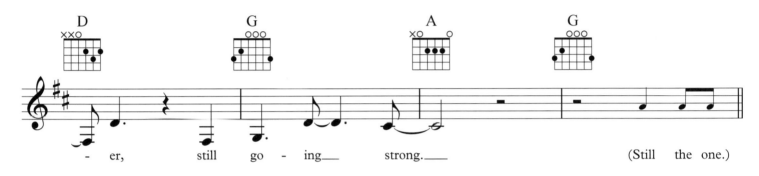

- er, still go - ing___ strong.___ (Still the one.)

Chorus

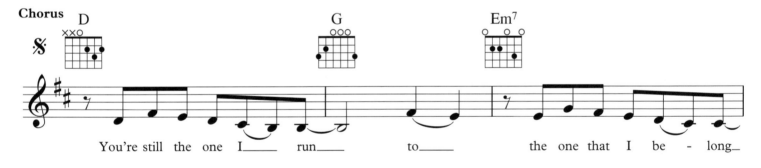

You're still the one I___ run___ to___ the one that I be - long___

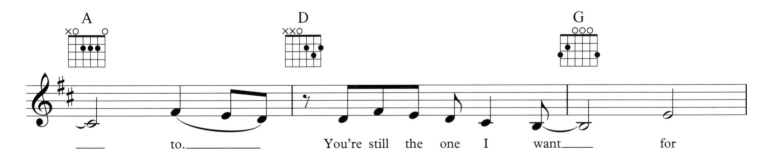

___ to.___ You're still the one I want___ for

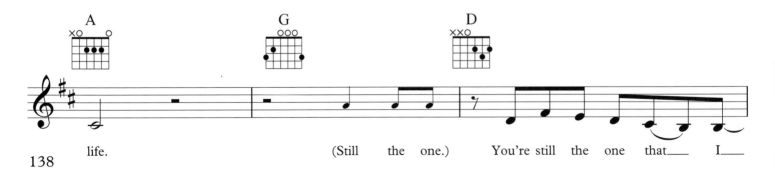

life. (Still the one.) You're still the one that___ I___

love,___ the on - ly one I___ dream___ of,_____

you're still the one I kiss good

1. **2.**

To Coda ⊕

night. You're still___ the one.

D.S. al Coda

(Still the one.)

⊕ *Coda*

I'm so glad we made___ it,

look how far___ we've come my ba - by.

Yesterday

Words & Music by John Lennon & Paul McCartney

Picking style:

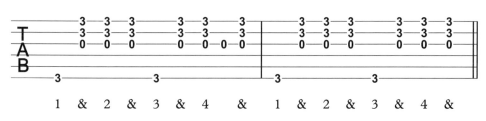

To match original recording, tune down one tone.

Intro

Verse

1. Yes - ter - day, all my trou - bles seemed so far a - way,

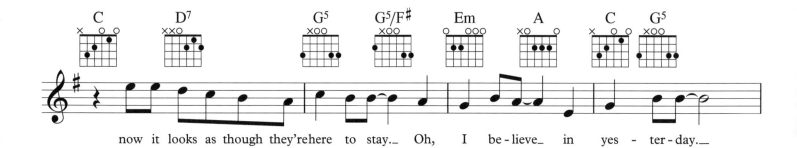

now it looks as though they're here to stay. Oh, I be - lieve_ in yes - ter - day._

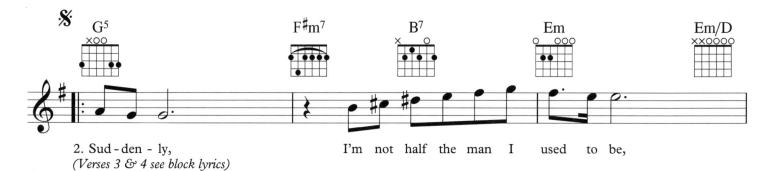

2. Sud - den - ly, I'm not half the man I used to be,
(Verses 3 & 4 see block lyrics)

Verses 3 & 4:
Yesterday, love was such an easy game to play,
Now I need a place to hide away.
Oh, I believe in yesterday.

You've Got A Friend

Words & Music by Carole King

Picking style:

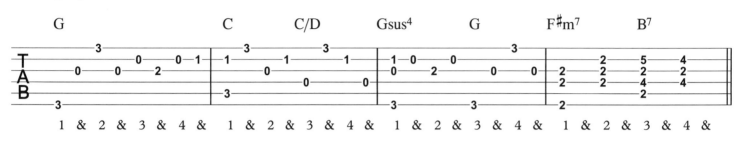

Capo: Fret 2

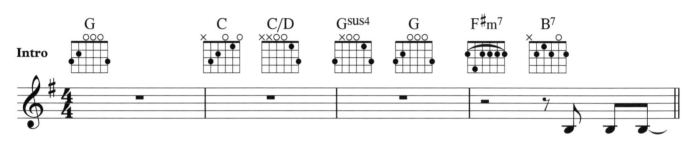

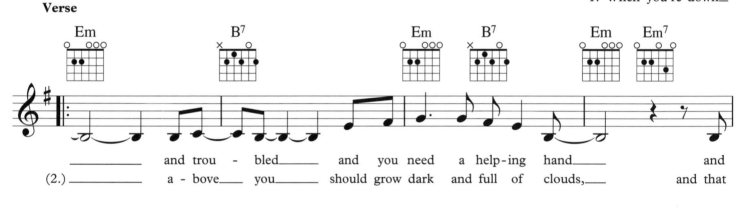

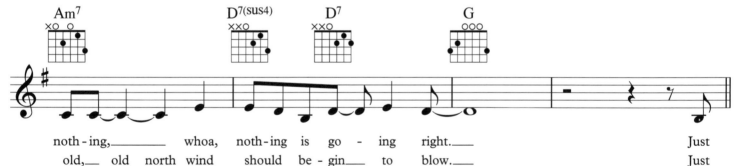

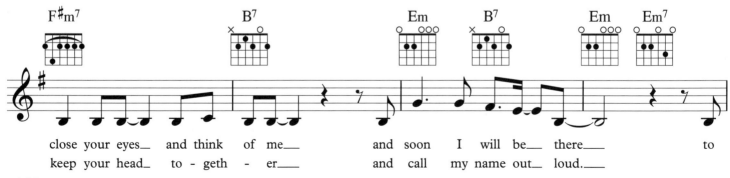

brigh-ten up___ e - ven your dark - est nights.___
Soon you'll hear me knock - ing_____ on__ your door.___

You just call___

Chorus

___ out my name,___ and you know___ wher-ev- er I am,___ I'll come run-

- ning___ to see you a - gain.___

Win - ter, spring, sum-mer, or fall,_____ all you have to do is call_____

To Coda **1.**

___ and I'll be there,__ yes I___ will.___ You've got a friend.___

143

123456789